Grégoire Denis

All about Zero Trust Networks

Grégoire Denis

All about Zero Trust Networks

Building secure systems based on zero-trust networks

ScienciaScripts

Imprint

Any brand names and product names mentioned in this book are subject to trademark, brand or patent protection and are trademarks or registered trademarks of their respective holders. The use of brand names, product names, common names, trade names, product descriptions etc. even without a particular marking in this work is in no way to be construed to mean that such names may be regarded as unrestricted in respect of trademark and brand protection legislation and could thus be used by anyone.

Cover image: www.ingimage.com

This book is a translation from the original published under ISBN 978-613-8-45948-4.

Publisher:
Sciencia Scripts
is a trademark of
Dodo Books Indian Ocean Ltd., member of the OmniScriptum S.R.L Publishing group
str. A.Russo 15, of. 61, Chisinau-2068, Republic of Moldova Europe
Printed at: see last page
ISBN: 978-620-4-09617-9

Table of Contents

Preface

Thank you for choosing to read this book! Building trusted systems in hostile networks has been my passion for many years. In building and designing such systems, I have seen a frustration in the pace of progress toward solving some of the most fundamental security problems that plague our industry. I would love to see the industry move more aggressively towards building the types of systems that strive to solve these problems.

To this end, I propose that the world adopt a new position with respect to the creation and maintenance of secure computer networks. Rather than being something that is overlaid, considered only after some value has been built, security must be fundamentally imbued with the operation of the system itself. It must be ubiquitous, enabling rather than constraining operation. As such, this book presents a collection of design patterns and considerations that, when taken into account, can produce systems that are resistant to the vast majority of modern attack vectors.

This collection, when considered as a whole, is known as the zero-trust model. In this model, nothing is taken for granted, and every access request - whether made by a customer in a coffee shop or a server in the data center - is rigorously vetted and proven to be authorized. Adopting this model virtually eliminates lateral movement, VPN headaches, and centralized firewall management overhead. It's a very different model indeed; one that I believe represents the future of network and infrastructure security design.

Security is a complex and constantly evolving field of engineering. Working on it requires a deep understanding of many layers of a system and how bugs or weaknesses in those layers can allow an attacker to subvert access controls and protections. While this makes defending a system difficult, it's also a lot of fun to learn! I hope you enjoy learning about it as much!

Who should read this book?

Have you found the overhead of centralized firewalls to be restrictive? Perhaps you've even found their operation to be inefficient? Have you struggled with VPN headaches, TLS configuration in a myriad of applications and languages, or compliance and auditing difficulties? These issues are just a small subset of those addressed by the zero trust model. If you find yourself thinking that there must be a better way, then you're in luck - this book is for you.

Network engineers, security engineers, CTOs (Chief Technology Officers) and everyone in between can benefit from learning without trust. Even without specialized skills, many of the principles included can be clearly understood, helping leaders make decisions that move them closer to achieving the zero-trust model, gradually improving their overall security posture.

In addition, readers experienced in using configuration management systems will see the opportunity to use these same ideas to build a more secure and operational networked system - one in which resources are secure by default. They will be interested in how automation systems can enable a new network design that can more easily enforce accurate security controls.

Finally, this book also explores the design of zero mature trust, allowing those who have already incorporated the basic philosophies to enhance the robustness of their security systems.

Zero Trust Networks today

The zero trust model was conceived by John Kindervag of Forrester in 2010. He has worked for many years to define architectural models and guidance for building zero-trust networks and has advised many large enterprises on improving their security. John was, and still is, an important figure in the field. His work in the area has greatly informed our understanding of the state of the union, and we thank him for popularizing zero trust during his formative years.

Today's Zero Trust networks are largely built using off-the-shelf software components with custom software to integrate the components in innovative ways. Therefore, as you read this, be aware that deploying this type of system is not as simple as installing and configuring ready-made hardware or software.

One could argue that the lack of easily deployable components that work well together is an opportunity. A suite of open source tools could help the adoption of zero trust networks.

Browse this book

This book is organized as follows: - Chapters 1 and 2 discuss the fundamental concepts involved in a zero-trust network.

- Chapters 3 and 4 explore new concepts commonly observed in mature zero trust networks: network agents and trust engines.

- Chapters 5-8 detail how trust is established between actors in a network. Much of this content focuses on existing technology that could be useful even in a traditional network security model.

- Chapter 9 brings all this content together to discuss how you might begin to build your own zero-trust network.

- Chapter 10 examines the zero confidence model from an adversarial view. It explores potential weaknesses, discussing those that are well mitigated and those that are not.

Acknowledgements

I would like to thank my friends Anthony Basquin and Amélie Delcourt for their help and advice during the writing process.

I would also like to thank my Father, Mother and Sister for their support. I found your comments invaluable and appreciate the time you took to read the initial drafts.

Chapter 1:
Zero Trust fundamentals

Today it is difficult for us to know who to trust. Can we be sure that our internet traffic is not bugged? Certainly not! What about our provider who installed the fiber? Or that contract technician who was in our datacenter yesterday working on the cabling?

Whistleblowers like Edward Snowden and Mark Klein have revealed the tenacity of government spying. The world was shocked when it was revealed that governments have been infiltrating data centers. But why? Isn't that exactly what we would do in their place? Especially if we knew the traffic wasn't encrypted.

The assumption that systems and traffic in a data center can be trusted is wrong. Modern networks and usage patterns no longer echo those that made perimeter defense logical years ago. As a result, moving freely through a secure infrastructure is often trivial once a single host or link has been compromised.

Zero Trust aims to solve the problems inherent in the trust we have in the network. Instead, it is possible to secure communication and access to the network in such an efficient way that the physical security of the transport layer can be reasonably neglected. Needless to say, this is a noble goal. The good news is that we have very good cryptography these days and, given good automation systems, this vision is actually achievable.

What is a zero trust network?

A zero trust network is based on 5 fundamental assertions:
- The network is always considered compromised (hostile).
- External and internal threats exist in the network at all times.
- Network location is not sufficient to decide trust in a network.
- Every device, user and network flow is authenticated and authorized.
- Policies should be dynamic and calculated from as many data sources as possible.

Traditional network security architecture divides different networks (or pieces of a single network) into zones, contained by one or more firewalls. Each zone is assigned a certain level of trust, which determines which network resources are allowed to be accessed. This model provides a very strong defense in depth. For example, resources deemed more risky, such as web servers facing the public Internet, are placed in an exclusion zone (often called a DMZ), where traffic can be closely monitored and controlled. Such an approach results in an architecture similar to some you may have seen before, such as the one shown in the following figure:

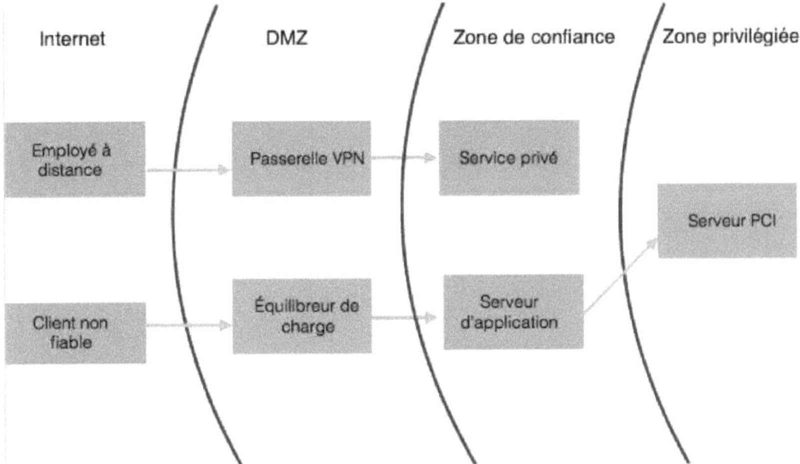

Figure 1-1

The zero trust model turns this diagram upside down. Placing the stopgaps in the network is a step forward from the designs of yesteryear, but it misses a lot in the modern cyberattack landscape. There are several disadvantages:

- Lack of intra-zone traffic inspection
- Lack of flexibility in host placement (both physical and logical)
- Single points of failure

> It should be noted that if the network location requirements are removed, the need for a VPN is also removed. A VPN allows a user to authenticate to receive an IP address on a remote network. Traffic is then tunneled from the device to the remote network, where it is **encapsulated** and routed. This is the biggest backdoor that no one suspects.

If we instead declare that the network location is worthless, VPN is suddenly rendered obsolete, along with many other modern network constructs. Of course, this mandate requires pushing the application as far to the edge of the network as possible, but at the same time relieves the kernel of such responsibility. In addition, stateful firewalls exist in all major operating systems, and advances in switching and routing have opened the possibility of installing advanced capabilities at the edge. All of these advantages combine to form one conclusion: the time is right for a paradigm shift.

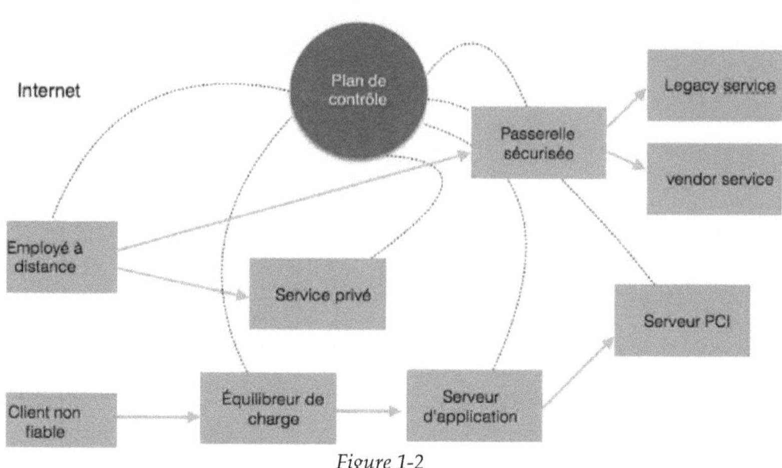

Figure 1-2

By leveraging the application of distributed policy and applying zero-trust principles, we can produce a design similar to that shown in the following figure.

Presentation of the zero confidence control plan

The support system is known as the control plane, while most other elements are called the data plane, which the control plane coordinates and configures. Requests for access to protected resources are first made through the control plane, where the device and user must be authenticated and authorized. A refined policy can be applied at this layer, perhaps based on role in the organization, time of day or device type. Access to more secure resources may also require stronger authentication.

Once the control plane has decided that the request will be allowed, it dynamically configures the data plane to accept traffic from that client (and only that client). In addition, it can coordinate the details of an encrypted tunnel between the requester and the resource. This can include temporary one-time credentials, keys and ephemeral port numbers.

While some compromises can be made based on these measures, the basic idea is that an authoritative source, or trusted third party, has the ability to authenticate, authorize and coordinate access in real time, based on various inputs.

Evolution of the perimeter model

The traditional architecture described here is often referred to as the perimeter model, after the castle-wall approach used in physical security. This approach protects sensitive objects by building lines of defense that an intruder must penetrate before gaining access.

Unfortunately, this approach is fundamentally flawed in the context of computer networks and is no longer sufficient. To understand the failure, it is useful to recall how the current model was developed.

Global IP address space management

The journey to the perimeter model began with address assignment. Networks were connected at an ever-increasing rate in the early days of the Internet. If it wasn't connected to the Internet (remember, the Internet wasn't ubiquitous back then), it was connected to another business unit, another company, or perhaps a research network. Of course, IP addresses have to be unique within a given IP network, and if network operators were unlucky enough to have overlapping ranges, they would have a lot of work to do to change them all. **If the network you are connecting to is the Internet, your addresses must be globally unique**. So clearly some coordination is needed here.

The Internet Assigned Numbers Authority (IANA), formally established in 1998, is the body that now provides coordination. Prior to the creation of IANA, this responsibility was held by Jon Postel, who created the Internet map shown in Figure 1-3. He was the authoritative source for IP address ownership records, and if you wanted to ensure that your IP addresses were globally unique, you registered with him. At that point, everyone was encouraged to register for the IP address space, even if the network being registered was not connected to the Internet. The assumption was that even if a network was not connected now, it would probably be connected to another network at some point.

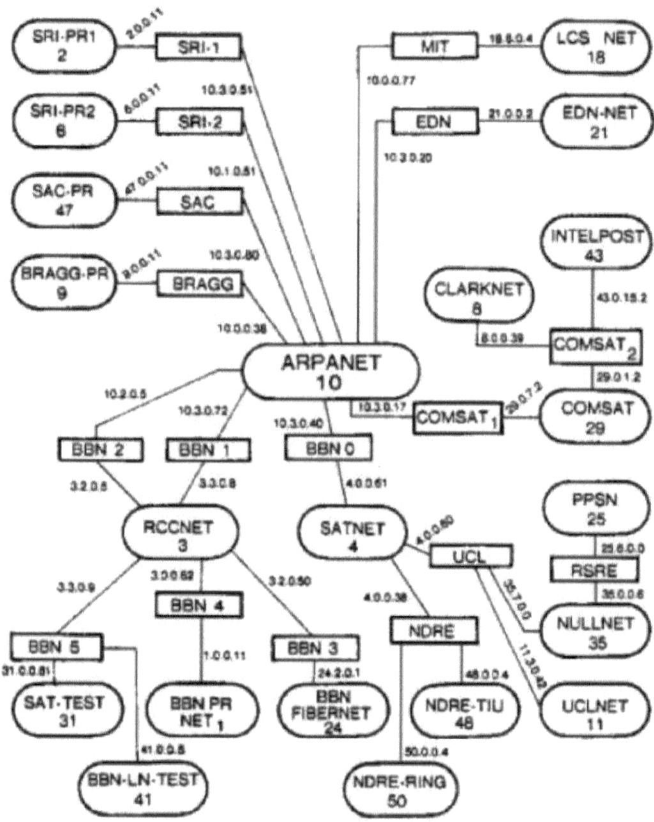

Figure 1-3

Birth of the private IP address space

As IP adoption grew in the late 1980s and early 1990s, frivolous use of address space became a serious concern. Many instances of truly isolated networks with large IP address space requirements began to emerge. Networks connecting ATMs and arrival/departure displays in large airports were presented as good examples. These networks have been considered truly isolated for a variety of reasons. Some devices may be isolated to meet security or privacy requirements (e.g. networks for ATMs). Some could be isolated because the scope of their function was so limited that wider access to the network was considered extremely unlikely (e.g., airport arrival and departure displays). RFC 1597, Address Assignment for Private Internet Networks, was introduced to address this public space problem.

In March 1994, **RFC 1597** announced that three IP network ranges had been reserved in IANA for general use in private networks: 10.0.0.0/8, 172.16.0.0/12 and 192.168.0.0/16. This has had the effect of slowing address exhaustion by ensuring that the address space of large private networks never exceeds these allocations. It also allowed network operators to use unique non-global addresses where and when they saw fit. It had another interesting effect, which persists today: **networks using private addresses are more secure, because they are basically unable to reach other networks, including the Internet.**

At the time, very few organizations (relatively speaking) had an Internet connection or presence, and as such, internal networks were frequently numbered with reserved slots. In addition, security measures were weak or non-existent because these networks were generally confined by the walls of a single organization.

Private networks connect to public networks

The number of interesting things on the Internet grew quite rapidly, and soon most organizations wanted at least some sort of presence. Email was one of the first examples of this. People wanted to be able to send and receive email, but that meant they needed a publicly accessible mail server, which of course meant they had to connect to the Internet somehow.

With established private networks, it was often the case that this mail server was the only server with an Internet connection. It had one network interface facing the Internet, and one facing the internal network. With this, the systems and people on the internal private network have the ability to send and receive email via their connected email server.

It was quickly realized that these servers had opened a physical Internet path into their private, secure network. If one of them was compromised, an attacker might be able to break into the private network, since the hosts could communicate with it. This realization required careful scrutiny of hosts and their network connections. **Network operators placed firewalls on both sides to limit communication and thwart potential attackers attempting to access internal systems from the Internet,** as shown in Figure 1-4. **With this step, the perimeter model was born. The internal network became the "secure" network and the pocket tightly controlled by external hosts became the demilitarized zone.**

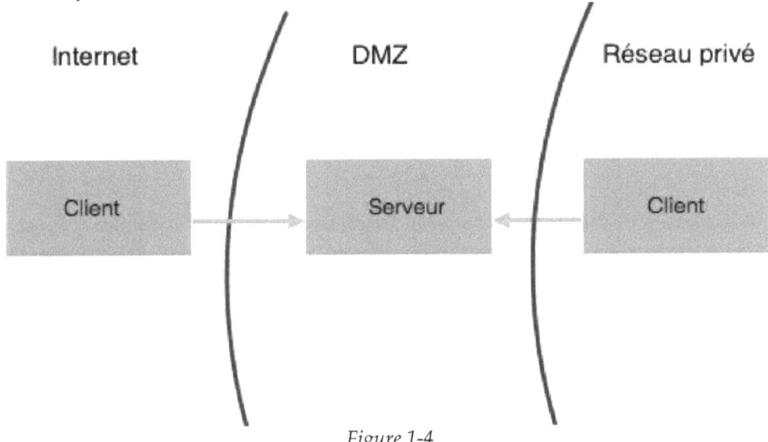

Figure 1-4

Birth of NAT

The number of Internet resources desired from internal networks was growing rapidly, and it was quickly becoming easier to grant general Internet access to internal resources than to maintain intermediate hosts for each desired application. NAT, or Network Address Translation, solved this problem well.

RFC 1631, the IP Network Address Translator, defines a standard for a network device capable of performing IP address translation at organizational boundaries. By maintaining a table that maps public IPs and ports to private ports, it allows devices on private networks to access arbitrary Internet resources. This lightweight mapping is application-independent, meaning that network operators no longer need to support Internet connectivity for particular applications; they only need to support Internet connectivity in general.

These NAT devices had an interesting property: because the IP mapping was all-in-one, incoming connections from the Internet could not access the internal private IP addresses without specifically configuring the NAT to handle this particular case. In this way, the devices had the same properties as a stateful firewall. **Real firewalls began to incorporate NAT features almost instantly, and the two became a single**, largely indistinguishable **function.** Supporting both network compatibility and stringent security controls, this device can be found at all organizational boundaries, as shown in Figure 1-5.

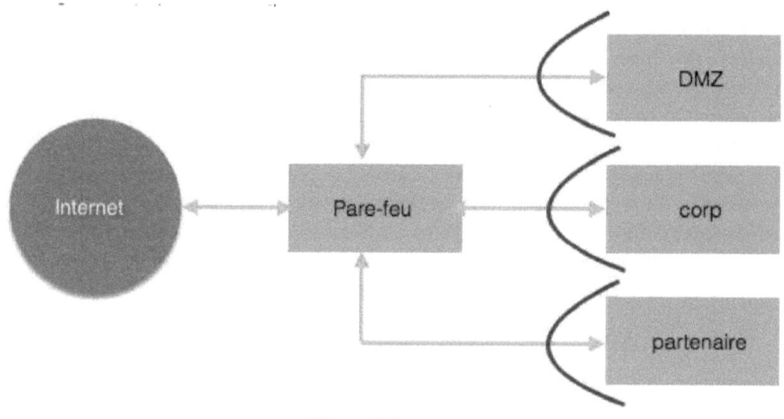

Figure 1-5

The contemporary perimeter model

With a firewall/NAT device between the internal network and the Internet, security zones are clearly formed. There is the internal "secure" zone, the demilitarized zone (DMZ) and the insecure zone (internet). If at some point in the future this organization were to interconnect with another, a device would be placed on this boundary in the same way. The neighboring organization is likely to become a new security zone, with special rules on what kind of traffic can pass from one to the other, just like the DMZ or the secure zone.

In hindsight, the progression can be seen in this way: we have gone from offline/private networks with only one or two hosts with Internet access to highly interconnected networks with security devices around the perimeter.

Evolution of the threat landscape

Even before the public Internet, communication with a remote computer system was highly desirable. This was generally done over the public telephone system. Users and computer systems could connect and, by encoding data in audible tones, acquire connectivity to the remote machine. These calling interfaces were the most common attack vector of the time, as physical access was much more difficult.

Once organizations had hosts connected to the Internet, the attacks moved from a telephone network to an Internet launch. This triggered a change in most attack dynamics. Inbound calls to calling interfaces blocked a phone line and were a notable event compared to a TCP connection from the Internet. It was much easier to have a secret presence on an IP network than on a system that needed to be called. Exploitation and brute force attempts could be conducted over long periods of time without arousing too much suspicion ... although an additional and more impactful capability was born out of this change: the malicious code could now listen in on Internet traffic.

In the late 1990s, the first Trojans (software) began to appear. Typically, a user would be tricked into installing the malware, which would then open a port and wait for incoming connections. The attacker could then connect to the open port and remotely control the target machine.

Soon after, people realized that it would be a good idea to protect these Internet-connected hosts. Hardware firewalls were the best way to do this (most operating systems didn't have a host-based firewall concept at that time). **They enforced the policy by ensuring that only "safe" whitelisted traffic was allowed from the Internet. If an administrator inadvertently installed something that exposed an open port (such as a Trojan horse), the firewall physically blocked connections to that port until it was explicitly configured to allow it.** Similarly, traffic to Internet servers inside the network could be controlled, ensuring that internal users could talk to them, but not vice versa. This prevented movement into the internal network by a potentially compromised DMZ host.

DMZ hosts were of course a prime target (due to their connectivity), although such strict controls on inbound and outbound traffic made it difficult to access an internal network via a DMZ.

This is where things took an interesting turn. NAT was introduced to grant Internet access to clients on internal networks. Partly because of the NAT mechanics and partly because of real security issues, there was always tight control over incoming traffic, although internal resources wishing to consume external resources could do so freely. There is **an important distinction to make when considering a network with NAT Internet access versus one without: the former has relaxed (if anything) outbound network policy**.

This dramatically transformed the network security model. Hosts on trusted internal networks could now communicate directly with untrusted Internet hosts, and the untrusted host was suddenly in a position to abuse the client trying to talk to it. Even worse, malicious code could then send messages to Internet hosts from the internal network. Today, we know that this is like "phoning home".

"Phone home" is an essential element of most modern attacks. It allows data to be exfiltrated from otherwise protected networks; but more importantly, since TCP is bidirectional, it also allows data to be injected.

A typical attack involves several steps, as shown in Figure 1-6. First, the attacker will compromise a single computer on the internal network by exploiting the user's browser when it visits a particular page, sending an e-mail with an attachment that exploits some local software, for example. The exploit carries a very small payload, just enough code to establish a connection with a remote Internet host and execute the code it receives in the response.

The payload downloads and installs the real malware, which will most often attempt to establish an additional connection to a remote Internet host controlled by the attacker. The attacker will use this connection to send commands to the malware, exfiltrate sensitive data, or even to obtain an interactive session. This "patient zero" can serve as a stepping stone, giving the attacker a host on the internal network from which to launch additional attacks.

Outbound security

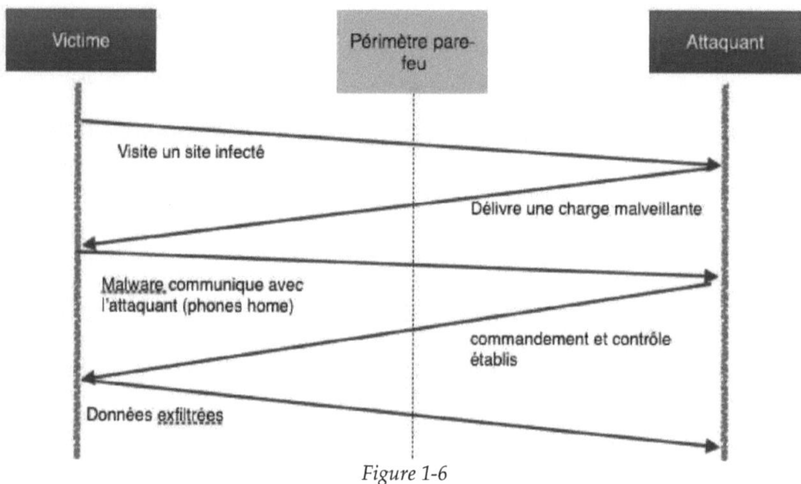

Figure 1-6

Outbound network security is a very effective mitigation measure against dial-up attacks, as the "phone home" can be detected and/or blocked. Often, however, the "phone home" is disguised as regular web traffic, perhaps even to networks that appear benign or "normal". Outbound security tight enough to stop these attacks will often cripple the ease of use of the web for users. This is a more realistic prospect for back-office systems.

The ability to launch attacks from hosts within an internal network is very powerful. **These hosts almost certainly have permission to talk to other hosts in the same security zone (lateral movement) and may even have access to conversations with hosts in more secure zones than their own. To this end, by first compromising a low-security zone on the internal network, an attacker can move through the network, eventually gaining access to high-security zones.**

If we take a step back, **we can see that this model very effectively undermines the perimeter security model**. The critical flaw allowing the attack to progress is subtle, but clear: security policies are defined by network zones, applied only at the zone boundaries, using nothing more than source and destination details.

Perimeter gaps

While the perimeter security model remains by far the most prevalent model, it is increasingly clear that the way we rely on it is flawed. Complex (and successful) attacks against networks with perfect perimeter security occur every day. **An attacker drops a remote access tool (or RAT) into your network via one of many methods, gains remote access, and starts moving laterally**. Perimeter firewalls have become the functional equivalent of building a wall around a city to keep out spies.

The problem lies in the architecture of the security zones in the network itself. **Imagine the following scenario**: You run a small e-commerce business. You have employees, internal systems (payroll, inventory, etc.) and a few servers to power your website. It's natural to start classifying the type of access these groups need: employees need access to internal systems, web servers need access to database servers, database servers don't need Internet access. Traditional network security would codify these groups as zones and then define which zone can access what, as shown in Figure 1-7. Of course, you actually have to enforce these policies; and since they are defined on a zone-by-zone basis, it makes sense to enforce them wherever one zone can carry traffic into another.

As you can imagine, there are **always exceptions to these generalized rules ...** they are, in fact, known as **firewall exceptions**. For example, your web developer may want to access the production web servers via SSH, or your HR representative may need access to the HR software database to perform audits. In these cases, an acceptable approach is to configure a firewall exception to allow traffic from that person's IP address to the particular server(s) in question.

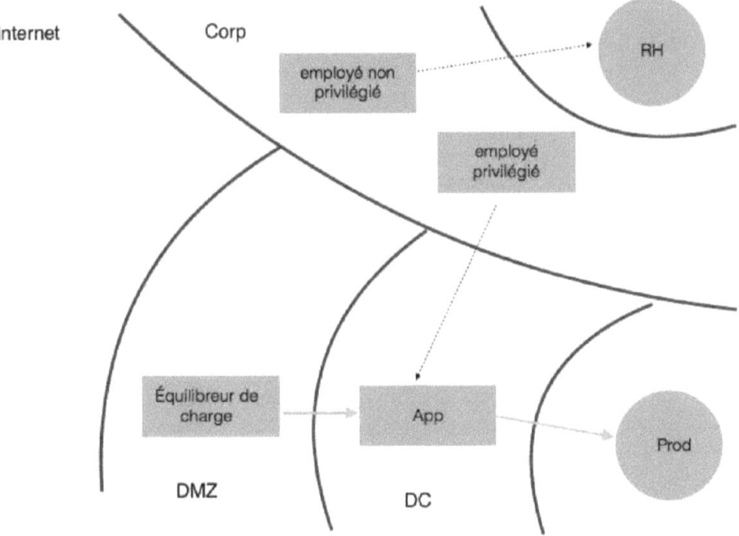

Figure 1-7

Now, let's imagine that your nemesis has hired a team of hackers. They want to get a look at your inventory and sales figures. The hackers send emails to every employee email address they can find on the Internet, posing as a discount code for a restaurant near the office. Effectively, one of them clicks on the link, allowing the hackers to install malware. The malware lodges itself and provides the attackers with a session on the now compromised employee's machine. Fortunately, he is only an intern and the level of access is limited.

They start searching the network and find that the company uses file sharing software on its network. Of all the employee computers on the network, none of them have the latest version and are vulnerable to an attack that was recently released. One by one, the hackers start looking for a computer with high access (this process can of course be more targeted if the attacker has advanced knowledge). Eventually, they come across your web developer's machine. A keylogger they install there, retrieves credentials to connect to the web server. They use SSH to connect to the server using the credentials they collected; and using the web developer's sudo privileges, they read the database password from the disk and connect to the database. They dump the contents of the database, download it and delete all the log files. If you're lucky, you might find that this breach has occurred. **They have accomplished their mission, as shown in Figure 1-8**.

Wait how? As you can see, many failures on many levels led to this breach, and while you might think this is a particularly contrived case, successful attacks like this are incredibly common. The most surprising part, however, too often goes unnoticed: what happened to all that network security? **Firewalls were meticulously placed, policies and exceptions were tightly bounded and very limited, everything was done from a network security perspective.** So where is the result?

Example of attack progression

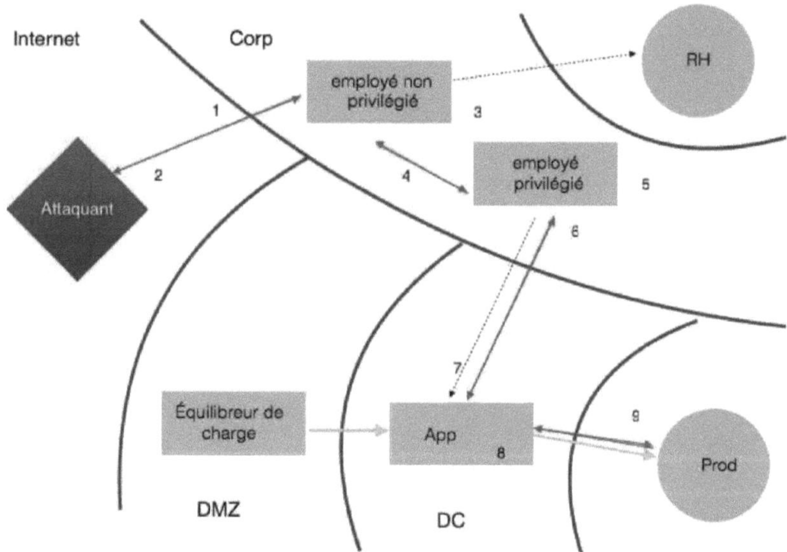

Figure 1-8

1. Employees targeted via phishing email
2. Compromised business machine
3. Lateral movement across the enterprise network
4. Preferred localized workstation
5. Local privilege escalation on the workstation - Keylogger installed
6. Stolen developer password
7. Compromised application host from a privileged workstation
8. Developer password used to elevate privileges on the application host
9. Stolen database credentials from the application
10. Database content exfiltrated via a compromised application host

Upon close examination, it is extremely obvious that this network security model is not sufficient. **Bypassing perimeter security is trivial with malware, and firewalls between zones consider nothing more than source and destination when making enforcement decisions**. While perimeters may still provide some value in network security, their role as the primary mechanism by which a network's security posture is defined must be reconsidered.

The first step, of course, is to research existing solutions. Obviously, the perimeter model is the accepted approach to securing a network, but that doesn't mean we don't have to learn better elsewhere. What is the worst possible scenario for network security? It turns out that there really is a level of absolutes to this question, and **the crucial point is trust**.

Where is the trust?

When considering options beyond the perimeter model, a clear understanding of what is trustworthy and what is not is required. The trust level defines a lower bound on the robustness of the required security protocols. Unfortunately, **robustness rarely exceeds what is required, so it is wise to trust as little as possible**. Once trust is built into a system, it can be very difficult to remove.

A zero-trust network is just as it sounds. **It is a completely untrusted network. Fortunately for us, we interact with such a network very often: the Internet.**

The Internet has taught us some valuable security lessons. Certainly, an operator will secure an Internet server very differently than it secures its locally accessible counterpart.

The zero trust model requires that all hosts be treated as if they were connected to the Internet. The networks in which they reside must be considered compromised and hostile. Only with this consideration can you begin to build secure communication. Since most operators have already built or maintained Internet systems, we at least have an idea of how to secure the IP in a way that is difficult to intercept or manipulate (and of course, how to secure these hosts). **Automation allows us to extend this level of security to all systems in our infrastructure.**

Automation as an enabler

Zero Trust networks do not require new protocols or libraries. They do, however, use existing technologies in innovative ways. The automation systems allow a zero trust network to be built and operated.

The interactions between the control plane and the data plane are the most critical points requiring automation. If the policy application cannot be updated dynamically, zero confidence will be unattainable, so it is essential that this process be automatic and fast.

There are several ways to achieve this automation. Purpose-built systems are the most ideal, although more mundane systems such as traditional configuration management can also accommodate this. **The widespread adoption of configuration management represents an important stepping stone to a network of zero trust, as these systems often maintain device inventories and are capable of automating the configuration of network enforcement in the data plane.**

Because modern configuration management systems can both maintain a device inventory and automate data plane configuration, they are well positioned to be a first step towards a mature Zero Trust network.

Perimeter vs. confidence 0

The perimeter and zero trust models are fundamentally different from each other. **The perimeter model attempts to build a wall between trusted and untrusted resources (i.e., the local network and the Internet). On the other hand, the zero-trust model throws in the towel and accepts the reality that "bad guys" are everywhere**. Rather than building walls to protect the "soft" bodies inside, it turns the entire population into a militia.

Current approaches to perimeter networks assign a certain level of trust to protected networks. This notion violates the zero trust model and leads to bad behavior. **Operators tend to let their guard down a bit when the network is "trustworthy" (they are human)**. Rarely are hosts that share a trust zone protected from themselves. Sharing a trust zone, after all, seems to imply that they have the same trust. Over time, we have learned that this assumption is false, and it is not only necessary to protect your hosts from the outside, but it is also necessary to protect them from each other.

Since the zero trust model assumes that the network is fully compromised, you must also assume that an attacker can communicate using any arbitrary IP address. Thus, protecting resources using IP addresses or physical location as an identifier is not sufficient. **All hosts, even those that share "trust zones", must provide proper identification**. Attackers are not limited to active attacks. They can still perform passive attacks in which they sniff your traffic to obtain sensitive information. **In this case, even host identification is not enough - strong encryption is also required.**

There are three key components in a Zero Trust network: user/application authentication, device authentication and approval. The first component has some duality due to the fact that not all actions are taken by users. So, in the case of an automated action (inside the data center, for example), we look at the qualities of the application in the same way that we normally look at the qualities of the user.

Authenticating and authorizing the device is just as important as doing so for the user/application. This is a feature rarely seen in services and resources protected by perimeter networks. It is often deployed using VPN or NAC technology, especially in more mature networks, but finding it between endpoints (as opposed to network intermediaries) is rare.

NAC as a perimeter technology

NAC, or Network Access Control, is a set of technologies designed to strongly authenticate devices for access to a sensitive network. These technologies, which include protocols such as 802.1X and the Trusted Network Connect (TNC) family, focus on access to a network rather than access to a service and, as such, are independent of the zero-trust model. An approach more consistent with the zero trust model would involve similar checks as close to the service as possible (something TNC can address). **While NAC can still be used in a Zero Trust network, it does not fulfill the Zero Trust device authentication requirement due to its distance from the remote endpoint.**

Finally, a "trust score" is calculated, and the application, device and score are linked to form an agent. The strategy is then applied against the agent to authorize the request. **The richness of the information contained in the agent allows for very flexible but precise access control**, which can be adapted to various conditions by including the score component in your policies.

If the request is allowed, the control plane signals the data plane to accept the incoming request. This action can also configure the encryption details. Encryption can be applied at the device level, the application level, or both. **At least one is required for privacy.**

With these authentication/authorization components, and the help of the control plane in coordinating the encrypted channels, we can assert that every flow on the network is authenticated and expected. Hosts and network devices drop traffic to which none of these components have been applied, ensuring that sensitive data can never leak. In addition, by logging every event and action in the control plane, network traffic can be easily audited on a flow-by-flow or request-by-request basis.

Perimeter networks can be found that have similar capabilities, although these capabilities are only applied at the perimeter. VPN tries to provide these qualities to secure access to an internal network, but the security stops as soon as your traffic reaches a VPN hub. It's obvious that operators know what Internet security looks like; they just fail to implement these strong measures throughout.

If one can imagine a network that applies these measures consistently, a brief thought experiment can shed much light on this new paradigm. Identity can be cryptographically proven, which means that the IP address of a given connection no longer matters (technically, you can still associate risk with it). With automation removing technical barriers, VPN is essentially obsolete. Private" networks don't mean anything special anymore: the hosts are as strict as on the Internet. Thinking critically about NAT and private address space, zero confidence makes it more obvious that security arguments in this regard are null and void.

Ultimately, the flaw in the perimeter model is the lack of universal protection and enforcement. **What we're really looking for are hard bodies, bodies that know how to verify credentials and speak in a way that can't be overheard**. Having hard bodies doesn't necessarily prevent you from also maintaining the security cells. In very sensitive facilities, this would still be encouraged. However, it raises the security bar enough that it is not unreasonable to reduce or remove these cells. **Combined with the fact that most of the zero-trust function can be done with transparency to the end user, the model seems to almost violate the security/convenience tradeoff**: stronger security, more convenience. Perhaps the convenience problem (or lack thereof) has been pushed onto the operators.

Applied to the cloud

Deploying infrastructure in the cloud presents many challenges, one of the most important being security. Zero Trust is perfectly suited for cloud deployments for one obvious reason: **you can't trust the network in a public cloud**! The ability to authenticate and secure communication without relying on IP addresses or the security of the connecting network means that compute resources can be almost commoditized.

Since zero-trust requires that every packet be encrypted, even within the same data center, operators do not have to worry about which packets traverse the Internet and which do not. This advantage is often underestimated.

The cognitive load associated with when, where, and how to encrypt traffic can be quite large, especially for developers who don't fully understand the underlying system. By eliminating the special cases, we can also eliminate the human error associated with them.

Some might argue that intra-data center encryption is excessive, even with the

reduction in cognitive load. History has proven otherwise. In large cloud providers like AWS, a single "region" consists of many data centers, with fiber links between them. The NSA was targeting precisely such links in 2013, and Internet backbone links even earlier in the rooms.

There are also risks in the network implementation of the provider itself. It is not impossible to think that there is a vulnerability where neighbors can see your traffic. A more likely case is network operators inspecting traffic during troubleshooting. Maybe the operator is honest, but what about the person who stole their laptop a few hours later with your captures on disk? **The unfortunate reality is that we can no longer assume that our traffic is protected from snooping or modification in the data center.**

Summary

This chapter explored the high-level concepts that led us to the zero-trust model. The zero trust model eliminates the perimeter model, which attempts to ensure that bad actors remain on the internal trust network. Instead, the zero-trust system recognizes that this approach is doomed to fail, and therefore assumes that bad actors are in the internal network and builds security mechanisms to guard against this threat.

To better understand why the perimeter model fails, we looked at how the perimeter model came to be. In the early days of the Internet, the network was fully routable. As the system evolved, some users identified areas of the network. Over time, this idea took shape and organizations modeled their security by protecting the private network of trust. Unfortunately, these private networks are not as isolated as the original private networks. The end result is a very porous perimeter, often breached in regular security incidents.

With the shared understanding of perimeter networks, we are able to contrast this design with the zero trust design. The zero-trust design carefully manages the trust in the system. These types of networks rely on automation to realistically manage security control systems that allow us to create a more dynamic and hardened system. We have introduced key concepts such as authentication of users, devices, and applications, as well as authorization of the combination of these components. We will discuss these concepts in more detail in the rest of this book.

Finally, we talked about how the shift to public cloud environments and the ubiquity of Internet connectivity has substantially changed the threat landscape. "Internal" networks are now increasingly shared and sufficiently abstracted, so end users don't quite understand when their data is traveling over more vulnerable wide area network links. The end result of this change is that data security is more important than ever when building new systems.

The next chapter will discuss the high-level concepts that need to be understood in order to build systems that can safely manage trust

Chapter 2: Managing trust

Trust management is perhaps the most important element of a zero trust network. We all know trust to some extent - you probably trust your family members, but not a stranger on the street, and certainly not a stranger who looks threatening. Why is that?

To begin with, you really know your family members. You know what they look like, where they live; perhaps you have known them all your life. There's no question who they are, and you're more likely to trust them on important matters than others.

A stranger, on the other hand, is someone completely unknown. You might see their face, and be able to tell some basic things about them, but you don't know where they live, and you don't know their story. They may seem perfectly nice, but you probably won't use them for important matters. Watch your stuff while you run to the bathroom? Sure. Make a short trip to the vending machine for you? Definitely not.

In the end, you simply take all the information you can get about the situation, a person, and everything you can know about them, and decide how reliable they are. The ATM race requires a very high level of trust, where keeping your things needs much less, but not zero.

You can't even trust yourself completely, but you can certainly trust that the actions you took were taken by you. **In this way, trust in a zero-trust network always comes from the operator**. Trust in a zero-trust network seems contradictory, although it is important to understand that when you have no inherent trust, you must find it somewhere and manage it carefully.

There is one small problem, however: the operator will not always be available to authorize and grant the trust! Fortunately, we know how to solve this problem - **we delegate the trust** as shown in Figure 2-1.

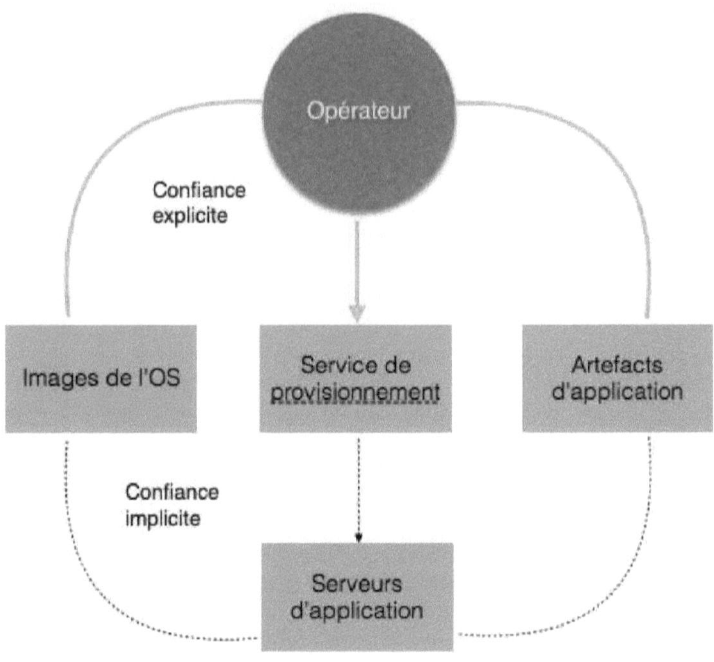

Figure 2-1

Trust delegation is important because it allows us to build automated systems that can scale up and operate securely and reliably with minimal human intervention. The trusted operator must assign a certain level of trust to a system, allowing it to act on the operator's behalf. A simple example of this is automatic scaling. You want your servers to configure to your needs, but how do you know that a new server is one of yours and not some other random server? The operator must delegate the responsibility to a provisioning system, giving it the ability to assign trust to new hosts and create new ones. In this way, we can say that we trust the new server to be ours, because the provisioning system has validated that it has issued the action to create it, and the provisioning system can prove that the operator has granted it the capability. **This flow of trust to the operator is often called a chain of trust, and the operator can be called a trust anchor.**

Threat models

Defining threat models is an important first step in designing a security architecture. A threat model lists potential attackers, their capabilities and resources, and their targets. Threat models typically define attackers in scope, rationally choosing to limit attacks from weaker adversaries before moving on to more difficult adversaries.

A well-defined threat model can be a useful tool for focusing security mitigation efforts. When building security systems, like most engineering exercises, there is a tendency to focus on the more sophisticated aspects of the engineering problem at the expense of the more tedious, yet important parts. This tendency is particularly worrisome in a security system, because the weakest link in the system is where attackers will quickly focus. Therefore, the threat model serves as a mechanism to focus our attention on a single threat and completely mitigate their attacks.

Threat models can also be useful in prioritizing security initiatives. Fighting state-level actors is pointless if a system's security measures are insufficient to defend against a simple brute force attack against a user's bad password. As such, it is important to start with simpler characters first when building a threat model.

Common threat models

There are many different techniques for threat modeling in the security field. Here are some of the most popular ones:
- STRIDE
- DREAD
- PASTA
- TRIKE
- VAST

The various threat modelling techniques provide different frameworks for exploring the threat space. Each has the same objective: to enumerate the threats to the system and to further enumerate the systems and processes for mitigating those threats.

Different threat models approach the problem from different angles. Some modeling systems may focus on the assets targeted by an attacker. Others may look at each software component in isolation and list all the attacks that could be applied to that system. Finally, some models may look at the system as a whole from the attacker's point of view: as an attacker, how could I approach this system? Each of these approaches has advantages and disadvantages. For a well-diversified mitigation strategy, an improvement of all three approaches is ideal.

If we were to look at the attacker-based threat modeling methodology, we are able to classify attackers into a list of increasing capabilities (from least threatening to most threatening):

1. Opportunistic strikers

So-called script kiddies, who are unsophisticated attackers, taking advantage of well-known vulnerabilities without a predetermined target

2. Targeted attacks

Attackers who create specialized attacks against a particular target. Phishing and industrial espionage could fall into this category.

3. Internal threats

An accredited but everyday user of a system. Contractors and non-privileged employees generally fall into this category.

4. Trusted Insider

A trusted system administrator.

5. Actor at the state level

Attackers supported by foreign or domestic governments and assumed to have extensive resources and positioning capabilities to attack a target. Threat categorization such as this is a useful exercise to focus the discussion around a particular level to mitigate. We will discuss Level Zero trusted targets in the next section.

Zero Trust's threat model

In RFC 3552, the Internet threat model is described. Zero Trust networks generally follow the Internet threat model when planning their security posture. While it is recommended to read the entire RFC, here is a relevant excerpt:

The Internet environment has a fairly well understood threat model. In general, we assume that the end systems involved in a protocol exchange have not themselves been compromised. **Protecting against an attack when one of the end systems has been compromised is extraordinarily difficult.** However, it is possible to design protocols that minimize the amount of damage done in these circumstances.

On the other hand, we assume that the attacker has almost complete control over the communication channel over which the end systems communicate. This means that the attacker can read any PDU (Protocol Data Unit) on the network and undetectably drop, modify, or inject packets into the network. This includes the ability to generate packets that appear to come from a trusted machine. **Thus, even if the end system you wish to communicate with is itself secure, the Internet environment provides no guarantee that packets claiming to come from that system are actually secure.**

Zero Trust networks, because of their control over endpoints in the network, expand the Internet threat model to account for endpoint compromises. The response to these threats is typically to first proactively harden systems against compromised peers, and then to facilitate the detection of these compromises. **Detection is facilitated by device analysis and behavioral analysis of individual device activity.** In addition, endpoint risk mitigation is achieved through frequent software upgrades on devices, frequent automated rotation of credentials, and in some cases, frequent rotation of the devices themselves.

An attacker with unlimited resources is essentially impossible to defend against, and zero-trust networks recognize this. The goal of a zero-trust network is not to defend against all adversaries, but rather the types of adversaries that are often seen in a hostile network.

Based on our previous discussion of attacker capabilities, **a zero-trust network generally attempts to mitigate attacks up to and including attacks from a "trusted insider" level of access.** Most organizations do not experience attacks beyond this level of sophistication. Developing mitigation measures against these attackers will defend against the vast majority of compromises and would be a dramatic improvement in the industry's security posture.

Zero Trust networks generally do not attempt to mitigate all state-level actors, although they do attempt to mitigate those who attempt to compromise their systems remotely. State-level actors are assumed to have large amounts of money, so many attacks that would be infeasible for smaller organizations are available to them. In addition, local governments have physical and legal access to many of the systems that organizations depend on to secure their networks.

Defending against these localized threats is extremely expensive, requiring dedicated physical hardware, and most untrusted networks consider extreme forms of attack (say, a vulnerability is inserted into a hypervisor that copies memory pages from a virtual machine) beyond the scope of the models. We need to be clear that while security best practices are still strongly encouraged, the zero-trust model only requires the security of information used to authenticate and authorize actions, such as disk-based credentials. Other endpoint requirements, such as full disk encryption, can be enforced via an additional policy.

Strong authentication

Knowing how much to trust someone is useless without being able to associate a real-life person with that identity you know you can trust. Humans have a lot of senses to determine if the person in front of them is who they think they are. It turns out that combinations of senses are hard to fool.

Computer systems, however, are not so lucky. It's more like talking to someone on the phone. You can listen to their voice, read the caller ID, ask them questions ... but you can't see them. So we're left with a challenge: how can we be reasonably assured that the person (or system) on the other end of the line is actually who they say they are?

Typically, operators examine the IP address of the remote system and request a password. Unfortunately, these methods alone are insufficient for a zero-trust network, where attackers can communicate from any IP address and insert themselves between you and the trusted remote host. Therefore, it is very important to use strong authentication on every flow in a zero-trust network.

SSL is anonymous

The most consumed TLS configuration validates that the client is talking to a trusted resource, but not that the resource is talking to a trusted client. This poses an obvious problem for zero-trust networks.

This further supports mutual authentication, in which the resource also validates the client. This is an important step in securing private resources; otherwise, the client device will not be authenticated. More information on zero-trust TLS configuration in "Mutually Authenticated TLS".

Certificates use two cryptographic keys: a public key and a private key. The public key is distributed and the private key is kept secret. The public key can encrypt data that the private key can decrypt, and vice versa, as shown in Figure 2-2. This allows them to prove the presence of the private key by correctly decrypting data encrypted by the well-known (and verifiable) public key.
In this way, the identity can be validated without ever revealing the secret.

Certificate-based authentication allows us to be sure that the person on the other end of the line has the private key, and also allows us to make sure that someone listening in can't steal the key and reuse it in the future. However, it still relies on a secret, something can be stolen. Not necessarily by eavesdropping, but perhaps by malware or physical theft.

So even if we can validate that the credentials are legitimate, we may not believe that they have been kept secret. For this reason, it is desirable to use multiple secrets, stored in different locations, which in combination allow access. With this approach, a potential attacker must steal several components.

The presence of multiple components prevents unauthorized access, but it is still conceivable that all these components could be stolen. Therefore, it is essential that all authentication information be time-stamped. Setting an expiration on credentials helps minimize the reach of lost or stolen keys and gives the operator the opportunity to reaffirm trust. The act of changing, or renewing, keys/passwords is known as credential rotation.

Rotation of credentials is essential to validate that no secrets have been stolen and to revoke them if necessary. Systems that use difficult or impossible to rotate keywords/passwords should be avoided at all costs, and when building new systems this should be considered early in the design process. The frequency of rotation of a particular degree is often inversely proportional to the cost of rotation.

Examples of costly secrets to rotate

- certificates requiring external coordination
- manually configured service accounts
- database passwords requiring downtime to reset

Trust authentication

We've talked a bit about certificates and public key cryptography. However, certificates alone do not solve the authentication problem.

For example, you can be assured that a remote entity is in possession of a private key by making an assertion using its public key.
But how do you get the public key to begin with? Of course, public keys don't have to be secret, but you still need a way to know that you have the right public key. Public Key Infrastructure, or PKI, defines a set of roles and responsibilities that are used to securely distribute and validate public keys in untrusted networks.
The purpose of a PKI is to allow unprivileged participants to validate the authenticity of their peers through an existing trust relationship with a mutual third party. A PKI leverages what is called a Registration Authority (RA) to bind an identity to a public key. This binding is embedded in the certificate, which is cryptographically signed by the trusted third party.

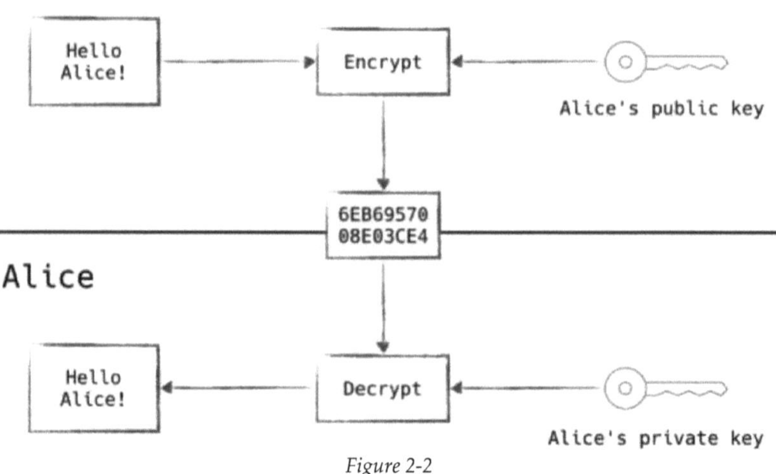

Figure 2-2

The signed certificate can then be presented to "prove" identity, provided the recipient trusts the same third party.

There are several types of PKI providers. The two most popular are Certificate Authorities (CAs) and Trusted Networks (TNs). The former relies on a signature chain that is ultimately rooted in the mutually trusted party. The latter allows systems to assert the validity of their peers, forming a network of mentions rather than a chain. Trust is then asserted by traversing the web until a trusted certificate is found. Although this approach is relatively widely used with PGP (Pretty Good Privacy) encryption, this book will focus on PKIs that employ a certificate authority whose popularity dwarfs the WoT provider.

What is a certification authority?

Certification authorities act as the trusted appendage of a certificate chain. They sign and publish public keys and their associated identities, allowing non-privileged entities to assert the validity of the binding through the signature.

CA certificates are used to represent the identity of the CA itself and it is the private key of the CA certificate that is used to sign client certificates. The CA certificate is well known and is used by the authenticating entity to validate the signature of the presented client certificate. This is where the trusted third party relationship exists, issuing and asserting the validity of digital certificates on behalf of clients.

The position of trusted third party is highly privileged. The CA must be protected at all costs, as its subversion would be catastrophic. Digital certificate standards such as X.509 certificates allow chaining of certificates, which allows the root CA to be taken offline. This is considered standard practice in CA-based PKI security. We will talk more about X.509 security in Chapter 5.

The importance of PKI to Zero Trust

All Zero Trust networks rely on PKI to prove identity across the network. As such, it acts as the foundation for identity authentication for the majority of transactions. Entities that can be authenticated with a digital certificate include:
- Peripherals
- Users
- Applications

Binding keys to entities

PKI can bind an identity to a public key, but what about a private key to the entity it is intended to identify? After all, it is the private key that we are really authenticating. It is important to keep the private key as close to the entity it was intended to represent as possible. The method by which this is done varies depending on the type of entity. For example, a user may store a private key on a smart card in their pocket, or a device may store a private key in an embedded security chip. We will discuss the methods that best fit the entities in Chapters 5, 6, and 7.

Given the number of certificates that a zero-trust network will issue, it is important to recognize the need for automation. If humans are required to process certificate signing requests, the procedure will be applied sparingly, thus weakening the overall system. That said, certificates deemed highly sensitive will likely want to retain a human approval process.

Private PKI vs. public PKI

Some might ask why this question. After all, public PKI has undeniable strengths. Factors such as existing utilities/tools, peer-reviewed security tools, and the promise of faster time-to-market are all attractive. There are, however, several drawbacks to public PKI that work against this principle. The first is cost.

The public PKI system relies on public trust authorities to validate digital certificates. These authorities are their own businesses and typically charge a fee for signing certificates. To the extent that a Zero Trust network has many certificates, the signing costs associated with public authorities can be prohibitive, especially when considering rotation policies.

Another major disadvantage of public PKI is that it is difficult to fully trust public authorities. There are many public trust CAs, operating in many countries. In a Zero Trust network using public PKI, any of these CAs may reduce the certificates approved by your network. Do you trust the laws and governments associated with all these CAs? Probably not. While there are mitigation methods here, such as pinning certificates or setting up a single public CA approval, it is still difficult to maintain trust in a disjointed organization.

Finally, flexibility and programmability may suffer when using public CAs. Public CAs are generally interested in maintaining public trust, so they use good security measures. This can include rules on how certificates are formed and what information can be placed on them. This can negatively affect zero-trust authentication in that it is often desirable to store site-specific metadata in the certificate, such as a role or user ID. In addition, not all public certificate authorities provide programmable interfaces, making automation difficult.

Public PKI strictly better than nothing

While the disadvantages associated with public PKI are significant and the author strongly discourages its use in a zero-trust network, they remain greater than no PKI at all. A well-automated PKI is the first step, and work will be needed in this area regardless of the PKI approach chosen. The good news is that if you choose to leverage public PKI initially, there is a clear way to move to private PKI if the risk becomes too great. However, this raises the question of whether it is even worth it, as automation of these resources will always be necessary.

Lesser privilege

The principle of least privilege is the idea that an entity should only have the privileges it needs to do its job. By granting only those permissions that are always required, as opposed to what is sometimes desired, the potential for abuse or misuse by a user or application is greatly reduced.

In the case of an application, this usually means running it under a service account, in a container or jail, etc. In the case of a human, it usually manifests as policies like "only engineers have access to the source code." Devices also need to be considered in this regard, though they often adopt the same policies as the user or application they were originally assigned to.

Privacy as a lesser privilege

The application of encryption in the name of privacy is an often overlooked application of least privilege. Who really needs access to the packet payload?

Another effect of this principle is that if you need high access, you keep those access privileges for as long as you need them. It's important to understand which actions require which privileges so that they can be granted only when appropriate. This goes beyond simple access control reviews.

This means that human users should spend most of their time performing actions using an unprivileged user account. When elevated privileges are required, the user should perform these actions under a separate account with higher privileges.

On a single machine, elevation of privileges is usually accomplished by performing an action that requires the user to authenticate. For example, on a Unix system, calling a command using the sudo command prompts the user to enter their password before running that command as a different role. In GUI environments, a dialog box may appear requiring the user's password before performing the risky operation. By requiring user interaction, the potential for malware to act on the user's behalf is (possibly) mitigated.

In a zero-trust network, users must operate in a similarly low-privilege mode on the network most of the time, elevating their permissions only when necessary to perform a sensitive operation. For example, an authenticated user can freely access the corporate directory or interact with project planning software. Access to a critical production system, however, should require additional confirmation that the user or the user's system is not compromised. For relatively low-risk actions, this elevation of privilege can be as simple as reprogramming the user's password, requesting a second factor token, or sending a push notification to the user's phone. For high-risk access, one may choose to require active confirmation from a peer via an out-of-band request.

Human-driven authentication

For particularly sensitive operations, an operator may rely on the coordination of several humans, requiring a number of people to be actively engaged in authenticating a particular action. Forcing authentication actions in the real world is a good way to ensure that a compromised system cannot interfere with them. Be careful, however the methods are expensive and will become ineffective if used too frequently.

Like users, applications must also be configured to have the fewest privileges necessary to operate on the network. Unfortunately, applications deployed in an enterprise environment are often given fairly broad access on the network. Either because of the difficulty of defining policies to control applications, or the assumption that compromised users are the most likely target, it has become common for the first step in configuring a machine to disable application security frameworks to secure the infrastructure.

Beyond the traditional consideration of privileges for users and applications, zero-trust networks also consider the privilege of the device on the network. It is the combination of the user or application and the device used that determines the level of privilege granted. By matching a user's privilege to the device used to access a resource, zero-trust networks can mitigate the effects of lost or compromised credentials. Chapter 3 will explore how this marriage of devices and users works in practice.

Traditional networks eventually converge on policies that remain relatively static. If new use cases requiring greater privilege emerge, the requester must push for a policy change; or, perhaps more frequently, he asks someone with greater privilege (a sysadmin, for example) to perform the operation for him. This static definition of policy has two problems. First, in more permissive organizations, privilege increases over time, which diminishes the benefit of less privilege. Second, in both permissive and restrictive organizations, administrators have greater access, which has led malicious actors to deliberately target system administrators with phishing attacks.

In contrast, a zero-trust network will use many attributes of activity on the network to determine a risk factor for the currently requested access. These attributes can be temporal (access outside of normal window activity for this user is more suspicious), geographic (access from a different location than the user), or behavioral (access to resources that the user would not normally access).

By considering all the details of an access attempt, determining whether or not the action is allowed can be more granular than a simple binary response. For example, access to a database by a given user from their normal location during normal business hours would be granted, but access from a new location at different business hours might require authentication of the user using an additional factor.

The ability to actively adjust access based on the risk of activity on a network is one of the many features that make untrusted networks secure. By dynamically adjusting policies and access, these networks are able to autonomously respond to known and unknown attacks from malicious actors.

Variable trust

Managing trust is perhaps the most difficult aspect of running a secure network. Choosing which privileges people and devices are allowed on the network is time consuming, constantly changing, and directly affects the security posture that the network presents. Given the importance of trust management, it is surprising how underdeployed network trust management systems are today.

The definition of trusted policies is usually left to the security engineers. Cloud systems may have managed policies, but these policies provide only basic isolation (e.g., super user, administrator, regular user) that experienced users typically exceed. Perhaps in part because of the difficulty of defining and maintaining them, requests to change existing policies may be met with resistance. Determining the impact of a policy change can be difficult, if caution pushes administrators toward the status quo, which can frustrate end users and overwhelm system administrators with change requests.

Policy assignment is also typically a manual effort. Users are assigned policies based on their responsibilities in the organization. This role-based policy system tends to produce large pools of trust in network administrators, weakening the overall security posture of the network. These trust pools have created a market for hackers to "hunt sysadmins", seeking out and compromising sysadmins. Perhaps the gold standard for a secure network is one without highly privileged system administrators.

These trust pools highlight the fundamental problem with trust management in traditional networks: policies are not dynamic enough to respond to threats to the network. Mature organizations will have some sort of auditing process in place for activities on their network, but audits can be performed too infrequently, and are frankly so tedious that it is difficult for humans to pass. How much damage can a malicious sysadmin do to a network before an audit discovers its behavior and mitigates it?

A more fruitful path might be to rethink the actor/trust relationship, recognizing that trust in a network is constantly evolving and is based on an actor's previous and current actions within the network.

This model of trust, considering all the actions of an actor and determining their reliability, is not new. Credit agencies have been offering this service for many years. Rather than having organizations such as retailers, financial institutions, or even an employer independently define and determine its trustworthiness, a credit agency can use real-world actions to assess an individual's trustworthiness. Consumer organizations can then use their credit score to decide how much to trust that person. In the case of a mortgage application, a person with a higher credit score will receive a better interest rate, which mitigates the risk to the lender. In the case of an employer, their credit score could be used as a signal for a hiring decision. On a case-by-case basis, these factors may seem arbitrary and opaque, but they serve a useful purpose; to provide a mechanism for defending a system against arbitrary threats by defining a policy based not only on specific details, but also on a constantly changing and evolving score.

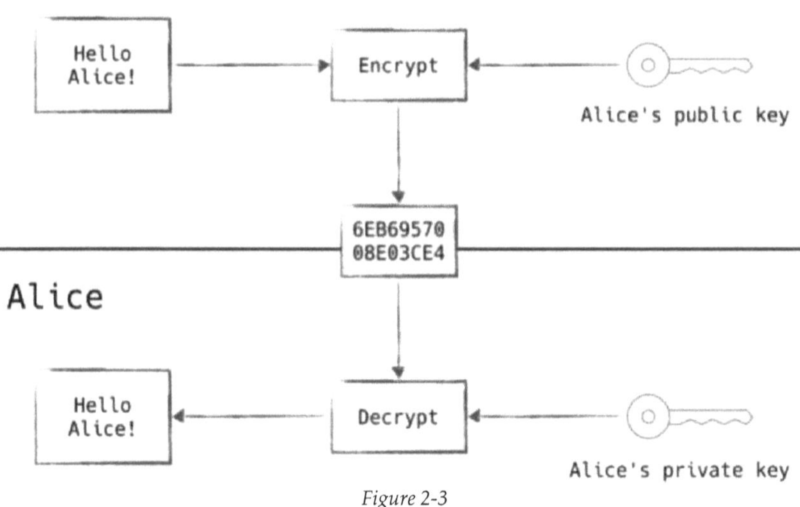

Figure 2-3

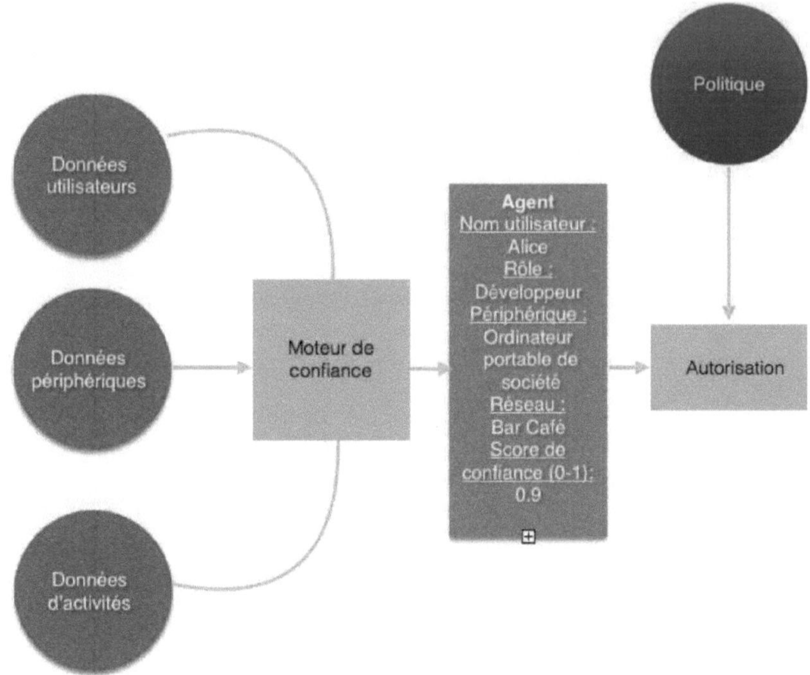

Figure 2-4

Monitoring of encrypted traffic

Since virtually all flows in a zero-trust network are encrypted, traditional traffic inspection methods do not work as well as expected. Instead, we limit ourselves to inspecting what we can see, which in most cases is the IP header and perhaps the next protocol header (like TCP in the case of TLS). However, if a load balancer or proxy is in the request path, it is possible to perform further inspection and authorization, as the application data will be exposed for review.

Clients start sessions as unapproved. They must accumulate trust through various mechanisms, accumulating enough to gain access to the service they request. Strong authentication proving that a device belongs to the company, for example, can accumulate a little trust, but not enough to allow access to the billing system. Providing the correct RSA token can give you a little more trust, enough to access the billing system when combined with the approval inferred from successful authentication.

A strong policy as a confidence booster

Things like score-based policies, which can affect the outcome of an authorization request based on a number of variables such as historical activity, greatly improve the security posture of a network compared to a static policy. Sessions that have been approved by these mechanisms may be more reliable than those that have not. In turn, we can rely (somewhat) less on user-based authentication methods to accumulate the trust needed to access a resource, thus improving the overall user experience.

Moving to a trust score model for policies is not without its drawbacks. The first hurdle is whether a single score is sufficient to secure all sensitive resources. In a system where an approval score may decrease based on user activity, a user's score may also increase based on a trustworthy activity history. Could it be possible for a persistent attacker to slowly build credibility in a system to gain more access?

Perhaps slowing down an attacker's progress by requiring a long period of "normal" behaviour would be enough to alleviate this concern, as an external audit would have a better chance of discovering the intruder. Another way to mitigate this problem is to expose multiple pieces of information to the control plane so that sensitive operations can require access from trusted locations and people. Binding a trust score to device and application metadata allows for flexible policies that can declare absolute requirements while capturing unknowns via the calculated trust score.

Loosening the coupling between security policy and a user's organizational role can be confusing and frustrating for end users. How can the system communicate to users that they are being denied access to certain sensitive resources from a coffee shop, but not from their home network? Perhaps we are presenting them with increasingly stringent authentication requirements? Should new members be required to live with inferior access for a period of time before their score indicates that they can have better access? Perhaps we'll gain additional confidence by having the user visit a technical support desk with the device in question. All are important points to consider. The route you take will vary from deployment to deployment.

Control plan vs. data plan

The distinction between the control plane and the data plane is a commonly used concept in network systems. The basic idea is that a network device has two logical domains with a clear interface between them. The data plane is the relatively simple layer that handles traffic on the network. Since this layer handles high traffic rates, its logic is kept simple and often passed to specialized hardware. The control plane, on the other hand, could be considered the brain of the network device. It is the layer to which system administrators apply the configuration and, therefore, changes more frequently as the policy evolves.

Since the control plane is so malleable, it is unable to handle the high network throughput. Therefore, the interface between the control plane and the data plane must be defined such that almost any policy behavior can be implemented on the data layer with infrequent requests to the control plane.

A zero-trust network also defines a clear separation between the control plane and the data plane. The data plane of such a network consists of the applications, firewall, proxies and routers that directly handle all traffic on the network. These systems, being in the path of all connections, must quickly determine if traffic should be allowed. When you view the data plane as a whole, it has extensive access and exposure throughout the system. So it's important that services on the data plane can't take advantage of the privilege in the control plane. We will discuss control plane security in Chapter 4.

The control plane in a Zero Trust network consists of components that receive and process requests from data plane devices that wish to access (or grant access to) network resources, as shown in Figure 2-5. These components will inspect data about the requesting system to determine the riskiness of the action and review the relevant policy to determine the required trust. Once a determination is made, the systems in the data plane are flagged or reconfigured to grant the requested access.

The mechanism by which the control plane affects the change in the data plane is critically important. Since data plane systems are often the entry point for attackers into a network, the interface between it and the control plane must be clear, ensuring that it cannot be moved laterally in the network. The requests between the data plane and the control plane system are reliable. The control plane/data plane interface should resemble the user space/kernel interface, where interactions between these two systems are strongly isolated to prevent privilege escalation.

This concern with the interface between the control plane and the data plane contradicts another fundamental property of the control plane: the control plane is the trusted constituent for the entire network. Because of its extensive control over the behavior of the network, the trustworthiness of the control plane is critical. This need to have an actor on the network with a highly privileged role presents a number of interesting design requirements.

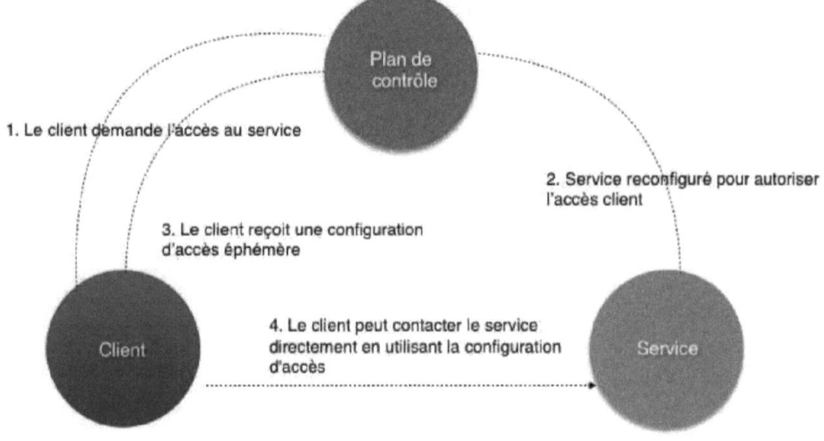

Figure 2-5

The first requirement is that the trust given by the control plane to another actor in the data plane must have limited real-time value. The trust should be temporary, requiring regular checks between the giver and receiver of the trust to ensure that the continued trust is reasonable. When implementing this principle, leased access tokens or short-lived certificates are the most appropriate solution. These leased access tokens must be validated not only in the data plane (e.g., when the control plane grants a token to an agent to move in the data plane), but also between the interaction between the data plane and the control plane. By limiting the window during which the data plane and the control plane can interact with a particular set of credentials, the possibility of physical attacks against the network is mitigated.

Summary

This chapter has discussed the critical systems and concepts needed to manage trust in a zero-trust network. Many of these ideas are common in traditional network security architectures, but it is important to lay the foundation for managing trust in a zero-trust network.

Trust comes from humans and flows into other systems via trust mechanisms that a computer can operate against. This approach makes logical sense: a system can only be considered trustworthy if the humans who use it are sure that it faithfully executes their wishes.

Security has often been seen as a set of best practices, passed down from one generation of engineers to the next. It is important to break out of this cycle, as each system is unique, so we discussed the idea of threat models. Threat models attempt to define the security posture of a system by enumerating the threats against the system and then defining the mitigating systems and processes that anticipate those threats. While a zero-trust network assumes a hostile environment, it is fundamentally rooted in the threat model, which makes sense for the system. We have listed several current threat modeling techniques so that readers can dig deeper. We have also discussed how the zero trust model is based on the Internet threat model and extends its reach to endpoints that are under the control of zero trust system administrators.

Trusting a system requires the use of strong authentication throughout the system. We discussed the importance of this type of authentication in a zero-trust network. We also briefly discussed how strong authentication can be achieved with today's technology. We will discuss these concepts in more detail in later chapters.

In order to effectively manage trust in a network, you must be able to positively identify trust information, especially in the case of authentication and identity. Public Key Infrastructure (or PKI) provides the best methods we have today for asserting validity and trust in a presented identity. We have discussed why PKI is important in a zero-trust network, the role of a Certificate Authority, and why a private PKI is preferred over a public PKI.

Least privilege is one of the key ideas in these types of networks. Instead of building an assumed secure network over which applications can communicate freely, the zero-trust model assumes that the network is untrusted, and therefore network components should have minimal privileges when communicating. We have explained what the concept of least privilege is and how it is similar and different from least privilege in autonomous systems.

One of the most exciting ideas in zero-trust networks is the idea of variable trust. Network policy has traditionally focused on which systems are allowed to communicate in any way. This binary policy framework results in policies that are either too tightly defined (creating human labor to continually adapt) or too loosely defined (resulting in security systems that claim very little). Moreover, a policy defined on the basis of concrete details of interactions will invariably get stuck in a cat-and-mouse game of adjusting the policy based on past threats.

The zero confidence model is based on the idea of variable confidence, a numerical value representing the level of confidence in a component. The policy can then be written with respect to this number, effectively capturing a number of conditions without complicating the policy with edge cases. By defining the policy in less concrete detail, and considering the trust score while making an authorization decision, authorization systems can adapt to new threats.

Zero Trust networks make a clear distinction between control plane systems and data plane systems. We have discussed at a high level how these two systems interact with each other to enable the expected communication through the network. In the following chapters, we will further flesh out the control and data plane systems that manage communication in the network.

The next chapter focuses on a fundamental entity in zero-trust networks used to authorize actions on the network.

Chapter 3: Network agents

Imagine you are in a security-conscious organization. Every employee is given a highly trained laptop to do their job. With today's work and personal life blending together, some also want to see their email and calendar on their phone. In this hypothetical organization, security teal applies detailed policy decisions based on the device the user is using to access a particular resource.

For example, it may be permissible to validate the code from the employee's laptop, but doing so from their phone would be rather strange. Since accessing the source code from a mobile device is significantly riskier than accessing it from a registered laptop, the organization blocks that access.

The story described here is a fairly typical application of zero-trust, in that multiple authentication and authorization factors take place, concerning both the user and the device. In this example, however, it is clear that one factor has influenced the other - a user who would "normally" have access to the source code will not have such access from their mobile device. In addition, this organization does not want authenticated users to commit to validating code from any approved device: they expect users to use their own device.

This marriage of user and device is a new concept that zero trust introduces, which we call a network agent. In a zero-trust network, it is not enough to treat the user and device separately, as strategies often need to consider both together to accurately enforce the desired behavior. By formally defining a network agent in the system, we are able to capture this relationship and use it to make strategic decisions.

This chapter will define what a network agent is and how it is used. In doing so, we will discuss the types of data that are included in an agent, some of which are potentially sensitive. Given the nature of this data, we will discuss when and how an agent should be exposed to data plane systems. A network agent, being a new concept, could benefit from standardization. We will explore the benefits of standardizing this agent.

What is an agent?

A network agent is the term given to the combination of known data about the actors in a network application, typically containing a user, an application and a device. Traditionally, these entities have been authorized separately, but zero-trust networks recognize that the strategy is best captured as a combination of all participants in a request. By authorizing the entire context of a request, the impact of credential theft is greatly mitigated.

A network agent is best thought of as an ephemeral entity formed on demand to evaluate a policy. The data used to form an agent (user or device information) is typically stored in persistent storage and queried to form an agent. When this data is queried, the union of data at that point in time is what we call an agent.

Agent Volatility

Some agent fields are made available specifically to mitigate active attacks, so they should change quickly compared to the infrequent changes IT organizations normally expect. Trust score systems can evaluate every request in the network, using this activity stream to update approval scores for users, applications, and devices. Therefore, for a trust score to mitigate a new attack, it must be updated as close to real time as possible.

In addition to changing data quickly, agents will often have sparse data. A device that is being booted is an example of a scenario where the agent will have less data when compared to a mature device. During the bootstrapping process, little is known about the device, but it still needs to interact with the enterprise infrastructure to perform tasks such as device registration and software installation. In this case, the boot device is not yet assigned to a user and may encounter problems if the policy expects an assigned user to be present in the agent. This scenario should be expected and reflected in the authorization policy.

Fragmented data is not only found in bootstrapping scenarios. Autonomous systems in a zero-trust network will frequently have sparse data compared to human-managed systems. These systems, for example, will likely not authenticate the user account under which the application runs, relying instead on the security of the configuration management system that created that user.

What's inside an agent?

The granularity of the data contained in an agent can vary depending on need and maturity. It can be as high level as a user's name or the manufacturer of a device, or as low level as serial numbers and location of residence or issue. It should be noted that more detailed data is more likely to have data cleanliness (reliability, integrity) issues that need to be addressed.

Agent data fields

The type of data stored in an agent can vary considerably in terms of presence and granularity. Some examples of data that can be found in an agent are:
- agent confidence score
- user confidence score
- role or user groups
- user's place of residence
- user authentication method
- device confidence score
- device manufacturer
- TPM manufacturer and version
- current location of the device
- IP address

Another consideration is whether or not the data in the agent is trusted. For example, device data populated during the provisioning process is more trusted than device data that is returned by an agent running on it. This difference in confidence stems from the difficulties in ensuring the accuracy and integrity of the reported information in the event that the device is compromised.

How is an agent used?

When you make an authorization decision in a zero-trust network, it is the agent that is authorized. While it is tempting to authorize the device and the user separately, this approach is not recommended. Since the agent is the entity that authorized, it is also the thing the policy is written against.

As mentioned in the previous section, the agent contains a lot of information. Thus, while more "traditional" authorization information such as IP address can still be used, using the agent also unlocks the use of "non-traditional" authorization information such as device type or city of residence. As such, the no-approval network policy is written against the agent as a whole, as opposed to creating a disjoint user and device policy.

Using an agent to drive an authorization policy encourages the author to consider the entire communication context. The marriage of user and device is very important in zero trust authorization decisions, and the co-location of data in an agent makes it difficult to ignore either. As with other parts of the Zero Trust architecture, lowering the barrier to entry is key, and co-locating data to facilitate comparisons between devices and users is no different.

An agent, being the main actor in the network, plays an additional role in the calculation of trust scores. The trust engine can use recorded actions, in addition to the data contained in the agent itself, to evaluate agents based on their trustworthiness. This trust score will then be exposed as an additional attribute on the agent against which most rules must be defined. We will talk more about how the trust score is calculated in the next chapter.

Not for authentication

It is important to understand the difference between authentication and authorization in the context of an agent? Agents serve only as authorization components and play no role in authentication. In fact, authentication is a precursor to agent formation and is typically performed separately for the user and the device. For example, devices can be authenticated with X.509 certificates, which can allow users to be authenticated via a traditional multi-factor approach.

After successful authentication, canonical identifiers for users and devices can be used to form an agent and its details. A device-specific certificate can be used as a canonical identifier for the device and, therefore, be used to fill in information such as device type or device owner. Similarly, a user name can be used as a search key to fill in information about users, such as their role in the company.

Typically, authentication is session-oriented, but in the case of authorization, it is better to be request-oriented. Therefore, caching the result of an authentication request is allowed, but caching an agent or the result of an authorization request is not recommended. This is because the details in the agent, which are used to make authorization decisions, can change rapidly depending on a number of factors, and it is desirable to make authorization decisions using the latest data. This is in contrast to authentication materials, which change much less frequently and do not directly affect the authorization itself.

Finally, the act of generating an agent should be as light as possible. If agent generation is expensive, it will discourage frequent authorization requests for performance reasons. We will talk more about how performance affects authorization in the next chapter.

Revoke authorization first, credentials second

Successful authentication involves proving one's identity to a remote system. This verified identity is then used to determine if the user actually has the right to access the resource in question (authorization). In the event that access needs to be revoked, update authorization is more effective than changing authentication information. This is doubly true when one considers that authentication results are typically cached and assigned to the session identifier. The act of committing an authenticated session is really an authorization decision.

How do you expose an agent?

The data contained in a network agent is potentially sensitive. Personally identifiable user information (e.g., name, address, phone number) will typically be present on the agent to facilitate detailed authorization decisions. This data must be handled with care to protect the privacy of users.

However, the sensitive nature of the data extends beyond the users. Device details can also be sensitive data when it falls into the hands of a determined attacker. An attacker with detailed knowledge of a user's device could use that data to create a targeted remote attack, or even learn a pattern of that user's physical location to steal the device.

To properly secure the details of the sensitive agent, the entire agent lifecycle must be contained in secure control plane systems, which are themselves highly secure. These systems must be logically and physically separate from the data plane systems, have clear boundaries, and be rarely changed.

Most policy decisions will be made in control plane systems, since agent data is needed to make these decisions. However, the authorization engine in the control plane is often not best placed to enforce application-centric policy, despite its ability to impose authorization on demand. This is especially true in user-oriented systems. Therefore, some agent details will need to be exposed to the data plane systems.

Let's look at an example. An administrative application stores details about all the customers of a particular company. This system exposes this data to employees based on their role within the company. A search feature allows employees to search the subset of data they have access to. The application must implement this logic and must have access to the user's role to do so.

In order to allow applications to implement their own authorization logic, agent details can be exposed to applications over a trusted communication channel. This can be as simple as injecting headers into network requests that pass through a reverse proxy. The proxy, being a zero-trust control plane system, can see the agent to apply its own authorization decisions and expose a subset of the data to the downstream application for further authorization.

Exposing agent details to the downstream application can also be useful to allow compatibility with pre-existing applications that have a rich authorization system.

This compatibility goal highlights that the agent details must be exposed to the application in a format preferred by the application. For third-party applications, the format of the agent data will vary. For first-party applications, a common structure for the agent data will facilitate system management.

No standard exists

A zero-trust network includes many systems that care about the agent. In order to make room for reusability in these systems, a normalization of the agent must take place. At the time of writing, most zero-trust networks consist of internally built systems; and while these systems have developed their own agent standards, a public standard would unlock the control plane, allowing components to be mixed and matched.

Rigidity and fluidity at the same time

Knowing the format of an agent and where to find particular data elements is very important when considering how and by what it will be consumed. The "coordinates" of some data must be fixed and well known in order to ensure consistency between control plane systems. A good analogy here is the schema of a relational database, which applications accessing the data must be aware of in order to extract the correct information.

This data compatibility is extremely important when it comes to implementing and maintaining zero trust control plane systems. Zero Trust networks, especially the more mature ones, are likely to build an agent from multiple systems and data sources. Without such a scheme, not only will it be difficult to standardize data, but it will also negatively contribute to the amount of effort required to introduce new control plane systems or agent data, which is considered critical to a mature zero trust network.

One thing to keep in mind, however, is that agent data is likely to be quite sparse, thanks to the almost inevitable data reliability issues encountered in source systems such as device inventories. The result is a "best effort" agent, where many fields may be unpopulated for one reason or another. Rather than seeking data reliability (a problem that only gets worse with scale), it is better to accept a reality and craft policy that understands that all data may not be present. Thus, while one can always require the presence of a particular data element in the agent, it is useful to think about other data elements in its absence.

Desirable standardization

One might ask how it would be possible to standardize a data format that is so closely tied to the organization that consumes it. After all, an agent is likely to contain types of information that relate to business logic or other proprietary/local information. Is normalization even feasible in such a case?

Fortunately, there are already standards defining data formats that behave in this way. One of the best examples is the Simple Network Management Protocol (SNMP) and its associated Management Information Base (MIB).

SNMP is a commonly used protocol for network device management, allowing devices to expose data to operators and management systems in a standard but flexible manner. The MIB component describes the format of the data itself, which is a collection of OIDs or object identifiers. Each OID describes (and is reserved for) a particular piece of data and is registered with ISO, the global standards body. This lends itself well to the widely accepted "coordinates" for some data.

Let's look at an example, shown in Figure 3-1, of a simplified set of nodes in an Object Identifier (OID) tree.

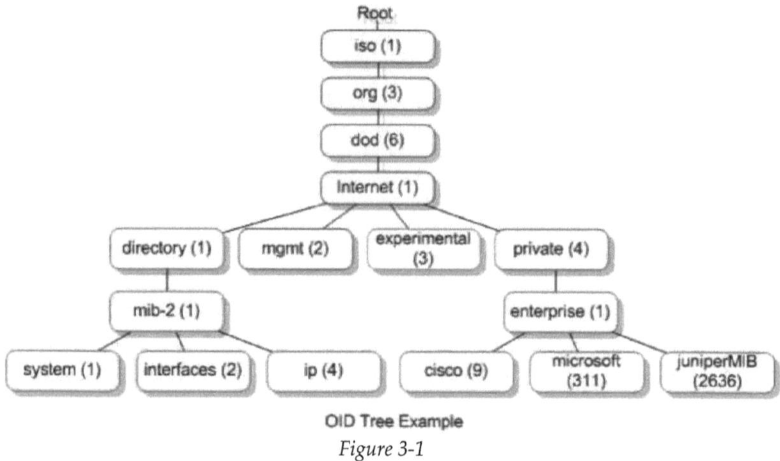

Figure 3-1

In this example, the "ip" node and its associated data will be processed as follows: 1.3.6.1.1.1.4. A MIB organizes and colors a set of OIDs. For example, a Cisco MIB may provide definitions for all OIDs in the 1.3.6.1.4.1.9 part of the tree, including user-readable descriptions.

Of course, this registered list can be expanded, and often pieces of OID space are carved out for organizations or manufacturers. In this way, an OID can be compared to an IP address, where an IP address globally identifies a computer system and an OID globally identifies a data item.

Unfortunately, there is no proper OID equivalent of the private IP address space, which would be useful for ad hoc or site-specific data. The best compromise available is to register for a private company number with IANA, which will give you a dedicated OID prefix for private use. Fortunately, such registration is free and with a few questions asked. Efforts have been made to create a private range similar to that found in IP. However, such efforts have failed.

Despite the lack of a truly free/private OID space for experimental or internal use, SNMP remains a useful analogy when considering agent standardization. It describes the format and packaging of a set of data - data that is easy to find and identify using its unique OIDs - and how that data can be transmitted and understood from one system to another.

In the meantime?

At the time of writing, Zero Trust Networks are still relatively new and the field is under active development. As such, no standard describing an agent exists today, and it will be some time before it can be ratified. In the meantime, agents take the form of a lesser resistance, given the needs of the implementer. Whether it's a JSON blob or a custom binary format, it's recommended to make sure that the data it contains is flexible and easily extensible. Loose typing or no typing should be preferred to strong typing, as the latter will make it more difficult to introduce new data and systems. Pluggable design patterns may help to move to a standardized agent in the future. However, this is far from mandatory and should not be pursued if it hinders the adoption of agent authorization in your network.

Summary

This chapter introduced the concept of a network agent, a new entity in a zero-trust network against which authorization decisions are made. The addition of this concept is essential to realize the benefits of a zero-trust network.

We have explored what happens in the creation of an agent. Agents contain rapidly changing data and often have unavailable or inconsistent data. Accepting that reality is important for success when introducing the agent concept.

Agents are used only to make authorization decisions. Authentication is a separate concern and the current authentication status is reflected in the properties of an agent. Control plane systems use the agent to authorize requests. These systems are primarily responsible for authorization in a zero-trust network, but they sometimes need to expose agent details to applications better positioned to implement accurate authorization decisions. We explored how to expose this data to applications while maintaining privacy.

The administration of the Zero Trust network is still very new and therefore a standard for network agents does not yet exist. Defining a standard would allow for better reuse and interoperability of zero trust systems, which would facilitate the adoption of this technology. We have discussed a possible approach to standardize the definition of an agent.

The next chapter will focus on the systems responsible for authorizing all requests in a zero trust network.

Chapter 4: Make authorization decisions

Authorization is arguably the most important process occurring in a zero trust network, and as such, making an authorization decision should not be taken lightly. Every flow and/or request will ultimately require a decision to be made.

The databases and supporting systems discussed here are the key systems that come together to influence these decisions. Together, they are the authority for access control and must therefore be rigorously isolated. Careful distinction must be made between these responsibilities, especially when deciding to reduce them into a single system, which should generally be avoided if possible.

The zero trust model is still very new and the field is evolving rapidly. Some of the content included in this chapter is considered state of the art at the time of writing. Known implementations still vary widely in their approaches, and most are not publicly available. That said, the main components and responsibilities are included.

With this in mind, this chapter will focus on the high-level architectural organization of the components required to make zero-trust authorization decisions, as well as how they fit together and apply those decisions.

Authorization architecture

The zero-trust authorization architecture consists of four main components, as shown in Figure 4-1 :
- Enforcement
- Policy Engine
- Trust Engine
- Data stores

These four components are distinct in their responsibilities and, therefore, we treat them as separate systems. From a safety perspective, it is highly desirable that these components be isolated from each other. These systems represent the practical jewels of the zero-trust security model, so special care must be taken to maintain and secure them. Carefully evaluate any proposal to consolidate these responsibilities into a single system.

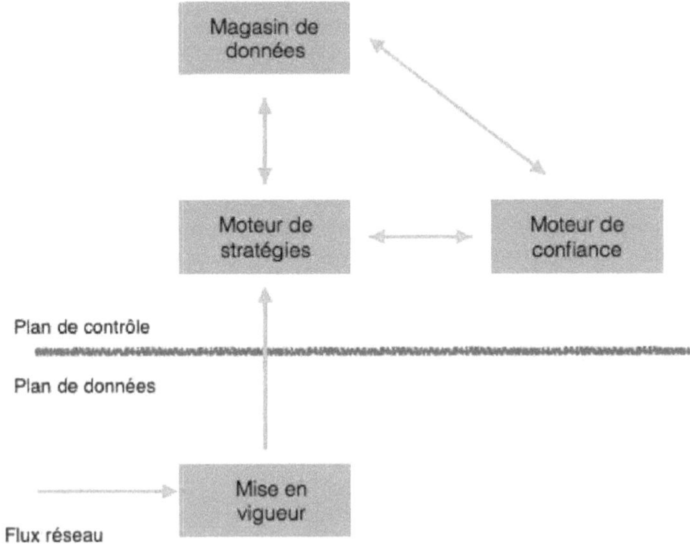

Figure 4-1

The execution component will exist in large numbers throughout the system and should be as close to the workload as possible. This is the one that actually affects the outcome of the authorization decision. It usually manifests itself as a load balancer, a proxy or even a firewall. This component interacts with the policy engine, which is the piece we use to make the actual decision. The application component ensures that clients are authenticated and passes the context of each flow/query to the policy engine. The policy engine compares the request and its context to the policy, and informs the application manager whether the request will be allowed or not.

The trust engine is operated by the policy engine for risk analysis purposes. It leverages multiple data sources to calculate a risk score, similar to a credit score. This score can be used to protect against unknowns, and keeps the policy strong and robust without complicating it with cases and signatures. It is used by the policy engine as an additional component to make an authorization decision. Google's BeyondCorp is widely recognized as the pioneer of this technology.

Finally, we have the various data stores that represent the source of truth for the data used to inform authorization. This data is used to paint a complete contextual picture of a particular stream/query, using small bits of authenticated data as the primary search keys (i.e., a username or device serial number).

These databases, whether user data, device data or other, are heavily leveraged by both the rules engine and the trust engine and represent the medium against which all decisions are measured.

Enforcement

The enforcement component (shown in Figure 4-2) is a natural place to start. It is on the "front line" of the authorization flow and is responsible for implementing the decisions made by the rest of the authorization system.

The application can be broken down into two main responsibilities. First, an interaction with the rules engine must take place. This is usually the authorization request itself (e.g., a load balancer has received a request and needs to know if it is authorized or not). The second is the actual installation and ongoing execution of the decision. Although these two responsibilities represent a single component in the zero-trust authorization architecture, you can choose whether they are performed together or separately.

How you choose to handle this will likely depend on your use case. For example, a proxy that knows the identity can call the rules engine to actively allow a request it has received and, in the same step, use the response to a service or reject the request. This is an example of handling concerns as unified. Alternatively, a pre-authorization daemon may receive a request for access to a particular service, which then calls the policy engine for authorization. Upon successful authorization, the daemon can manipulate local firewall rules to authorize the specific request. With this approach, we rely on "standard" enforcement mechanisms that are informed/scheduled by the trusted zero control plane. Note, however, that this approach requires a client-side "hook" to notify the control plane of the authorization request. This may or may not be acceptable, depending on the level of control of your devices and applications.

The placement of the application component is very important. Since it represents our control pointer in the data plane, we need to ensure that the application components are placed as close to the endpoints as possible. Otherwise, the trust can pool the execution component, compromising the security of the zero trust. Fortunately, the application component can be modeled as a client of any kind and applied generously throughout the system. This is in contrast to the rest of the authorization components, which are modeled as services.

Strategy engine

The rule engine is the component that has the power to make a decision. It compares the request from the application component with the policy to

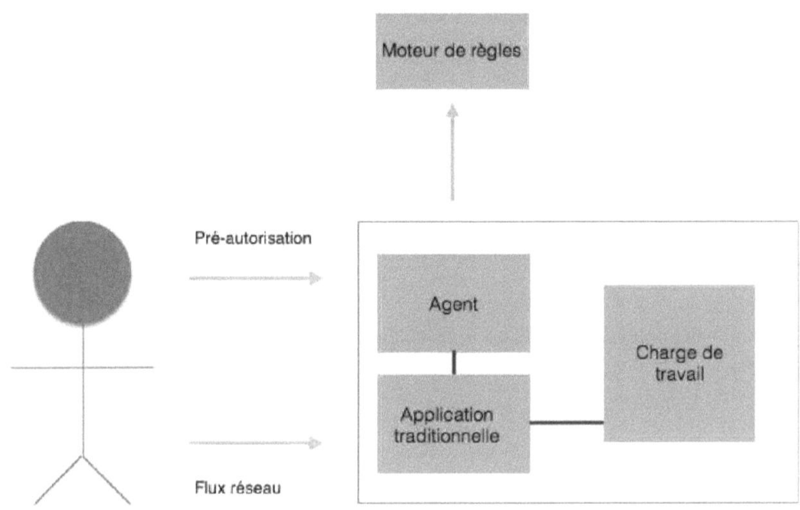

Figure 4-2

Determine whether the request is authorized or not. Once determined, the result is sent back to the execution document for actual execution.

The arrangement of the application layer and the rule engine allows for dynamic decisions to be made at a point in time, allowing for rapid revocation. As such, it is important that these components be considered separately and independently. This does not mean, however, that they cannot be co-located.

Depending on a number of factors, a policy engine may be found hosted side by side with the application mechanism. An example of this could be a load balancer that allows requests via inter-process communication (IPC) instead of a remote call. The most interesting advantage of this architecture is the lower latency to authorize the request. A low-latency authorization system allows fine-grained and comprehensive authorization of network activity; for example, individual HTTP requests could be authorized instead of the session-level authorization that is typically deployed.

It should be noted that it is best to maintain process-level isolation between the policy engine and the application layer. The application layer, located in the user's data path, is more exposed. Therefore, integrating the policy engine into the same process could expose it to unwanted risk. Deploying the policy engine as its own process prevents bugs in the application layer from compromising the policy engine.

What happened to RADIUS

The relationship between the policy engine and the enforcement layer is familiar to most network engineers. In 1997, the IETF ratified a standard describing the RADIUS protocol, which provides authentication, authorization and accounting for network services. RADIUS stands for Remote Authentication Dial-In User Service - the name alone indicates its age. While the protocol itself is hopelessly insecure (it uses MD5 for authenticity assertions), it is specifically written for the current test. What would it look like to use RADIUS between the application layer and the rules engine? RADIUS could be protected with other protocols discussed in this book, but it looks like a kludge (deemed a clumsy, crude solution). Perhaps there is an opportunity to create a RADIUS-like project that takes into account the reality of threats in current systems.

Storage of rules

Rules referenced by the rules engine must be stored. These policy rules are eventually loaded into the rules engine, but it is highly recommended that these rules be captured outside of the rules engine itself. Storing policy rules in a version control system is ideal and offers several advantages:
- policy changes can be tracked over time
- the rationale for the policy change is tracked in the version control system
- the current state of the expected policy can be validated against the mechanisms actual application

Many of these benefits have always been implemented through rigorous change management procedures. In this system, changes to the system configuration are requested and approved before they are finally implemented. The resulting change management log can be used to determine why the system is in the current state.

Moving policy definitions into version control is the logical conclusion of change management procedures when the system can be programmatically configured. Instead of relying on human system administrators to load the desired policy into the system, we can instead capture the policy as data that a program can read and apply. In many ways, the loading policy is similar to deployable software. Therefore, system administrators can use standard software development procedures (i.e. code reviews and promotion pipelines) to manage policy changes.

What makes good policy?

Policy in a zero-trust network is in some ways similar to traditional network security, and in other ways significantly different.

The zero-trust policy is still not standardized

The reality today is that zero trust policy is still not standardized in the same way as network-based policy. Therefore, defining the standard rule language used in a Zero Trust network is an excellent opportunity.

Let's look at what is similar first. A good policy in a zero-trust network is fine-grained. The level of granularity will vary depending on the maturity of the network, but the goal is a policy that is limited to the individual resource being secured. This is not much different from a traditional network security model that aims to segment the network to decrease the attack surface.

The Zero Trust model begins to diverge from traditional network security in the control mechanisms that are used to define policy. Instead of defining policy in terms of network implementation details (IP addresses and ranges), policy is better defined in terms of logical components in the network. These components will typically include:
- Network devices
- classes of peripheral termination points

- user roles

Defining policy from logical components that exist in the network allows the policy engine to calculate enforcement decisions based on its knowledge of the current state of the network. To put it concretely, a web service running on one server today might be on a different server tomorrow, or might even move between servers automatically as directed by a workload scheduler. The policy we define must be separated from these implementation details to accommodate this reality. An example of this policy from the Kubernetes project is shown in Figure 4-3.

Strategy in a zero-trust network also relies on trust scores to anticipate unknown attack vectors. By defining a policy with a trust score component, administrators are able to mitigate risks that otherwise cannot be captured with a specific policy. Therefore, most policies must include a trust score component. We will talk more about the score component in the next section.

No standard exists

Currently, mature zero trust networks implement their own policy language/format on a case-by-case basis, usually internally. Simpler Zero Trust networks may incorporate a policy into an existing structure, as in Figure 4-3. While this is generally acceptable, it is usually outdated as the network evolves and adds functionality. The benefits of a standardized / interoperable policy language can be clearly seen. However, such work remains an open research question.

The policy should not be based solely on the confidence score. The specific characteristics of the authorized request can also be part of the policy definition. An example of this might be: certain user roles should only have access to a particular service.

```
metadata:
  name: test-network-policy
  namespace: default
spec:
  podSelector:
   matchLabels:
      role: db
  ingress:
   - from:
      - namespaceSelector:
         matchLabels:
           project: myproject
      - podSelector:
         matchLabels:
           role: frontend
```

Figure 4-3

Who sets the policy?

The Zero Trust network policy needs to be refined, which can place an extraordinary burden on system administrators to keep the policy current. To help spread the configuration load, most organizations decide to distribute the policy definition across teams so that they can help maintain the policy for the services they own.

Opening up policy definition to an entire organization can present certain risks, such as well-meaning users creating overly broad policies, thereby increasing the attack surface of the system they intend to constrain. Zero trust systems rely on two organizational workflows to counter its exposure.

First, because the policy is typically stored under version control, having someone else review changes to the policy ensures that the changes are reflected. In addition, security teams can review changes and ask probing questions to ensure that the defined policy is as tight as possible. Since the policy is defined using logical intent instead of physical components, the policy will change less quickly than if it were defined in physical terms.

The second organizational measure used is to overlay a broad infrastructure policy with a refined policy. For example, an infrastructure group may rightly require that only a certain set of roles be allowed to accept traffic from the Internet. The infrastructure team will therefore define a policy that enforces this restriction, and no user-defined policy will be allowed to override it. Enforcement of this constraint can take several forms: an automated test of the proposed policy, or perhaps a policy engine that will simply reject overly broad policy assertions from untrusted sources. Such enforcement can also be useful for compliance and regulatory requirements.

Confidence-building engine

The trust engine is the system in a zero-trust network that performs a risk analysis against a particular request or action. The responsibility of this system is to produce a numerical assessment of the risk of allowing a particular request/action, which the policy engine uses to make a final authorization decision.

The trust engine frequently draws on data contained in authoritative inventor systems to verify an entity's attributes when calculating its score. A device inventory, for example, can provide the trust engine with information such as the last time a device was audited or whether it has a particular hardware security feature.

Creating a numerical risk assessment is a difficult task. A simple approach would be to define a set of ad hoc rules (for this purpose) that assess the risk of an entity. For example, a device that misses the latest software patches may have its score reduced. Similarly, a user that fails to authenticate all the time might have its trust score reduced.

Although ad hoc trust scoring can be simple to use, a statically defined set of rules will be insufficient to achieve the desired goal of defense against unexpected attacks. Therefore, in addition to using static rules, mature approval engines use machine learning techniques to derive an evaluation function.

Machine learning derives a scoring function by computing observable facts from a subset of activity data known as training data. The training data are raw observations that have been associated with trusted or unapproved entities. From this data, entities are extracted and used to derive a computer-generated scoring function. This scoring function, a model in machine learning terms, is then run on a data set that is in the same format as the training data. The resulting scores are compared to human-defined risk assessments, and the quality of the model can then be redefined based on its ability to correctly predict the risk of the analyzed data. A model that has sufficient accuracy can then be considered predictive of the risk of applications still unseen in the network.

While machine learning is increasingly used to solve difficult computational problems, it does not eliminate the need for more explicit rules in the trust engine. Whether due to the limitation of derived scoring models or the desired customization of the scoring function, trust engines typically use a mix of ad hoc scoring and machine learning methods.

Which entities are rated?

Deciding which components of a zero-trust network should be scored is an interesting consideration. Should scores be calculated for each individual entity (user, device and application), for the network agent as a whole or for both? Let's look at some scenarios.

Imagine that a user's credentials are brute forced by a malicious third party. Some systems will mitigate this threat by locking the user's account, which can present a denial-of-service attack against that particular user. If we were to negatively tag a user based on this activity, a zero-trust network would encounter the same problem. A better approach is to realize that we authenticate the network agent, and the attacker's network agent is neutralized, leaving the legitimate user's network agent intact. This scenario argues that the network agent is the entity that should be scored.

But simply tagging the network agent may not be sufficient against other attack vectors. Consider a device that has been associated with malicious activity. A user's network agent on this device may show no signs of malicious behavior, but the fact that the agent is trained with a suspected device should clearly impact the trust score for all requests from that device. This scenario strongly suggests that the device should be noted.

Finally, consider a malicious human user (the nefarious insider threat) uses multiple kiosk devices to exfiltrate trade secrets. We want the trust engine to recognize this behavior as the user traverses the devices and reflect the decreasing level of trust in their trust score for all future authorization decisions.

Again, we find that the network officer's rating alone is insufficient to mitigate common threats.

Overall, it seems that the right solution is to score both the network agent itself and the underlying entities that make up the agent. The scores can be exposed to the rules engine, which can choose the correct component(s) to allow based on the policy being written.

However, presenting so many scores to policy development can make the task of policy development more difficult and error-prone. In an ideal world, a single score would suffice, but this approach presents additional availability requirements on the trust engine. A system that attempts to create a single score would likely have to move to an online model, where the trust engine is queried interactively during policy making. The engine would be given some context about the request for authorization so that it can choose the best scoring function for that particular request. This design is clearly more complex to build and use. Also, for a policy where a system administrator wants to specifically target a particular component (e.g., only allow deployments from devices with a score greater than X), it seems rather round.

Exposing scores that are considered risky

While the scores assigned to entities in a zero-trust network are not considered confidential, it is important to avoid exposing the scores to the end users of the system. Seeing one's score could be a signal to potential attackers that they are increasing or decreasing their trust in the system. This desire to withhold information should be balanced by the frustration of end users' ability to understand how their actions affect their own trust in the system. A good compromise on the part of the fraud industry is to show scores to users infrequently, and to highlight the factors contributing to the determination of their score.

Data stores

The data stores used to make authorization decisions are simply the sources of truth for the current and past state of the system. Information from these data stores flows through the control plane systems, providing much of the basis on which authorization decisions are made, as shown in Figure 4-4.

We have already discussed the trust engine which leverages these data stores to produce a trust score, which in turn is taken into account by the policy engine. In this way, the information from the control plane data stores flowed through the authorization system, eventually reaching the policy engine where the decision was made.

These databases are used by the policy, both directly and indirectly, but may be useful to other systems that need authoritative data on the state of the network.

Zero Trust networks tend to have many data stores, organized by function. There are two main types: inventory and history. An inventory is a single source of consistent truth, recording the current state of the resource(s) it represents. An example is a user inventory that stores all user information, or a device inventory that records device information.

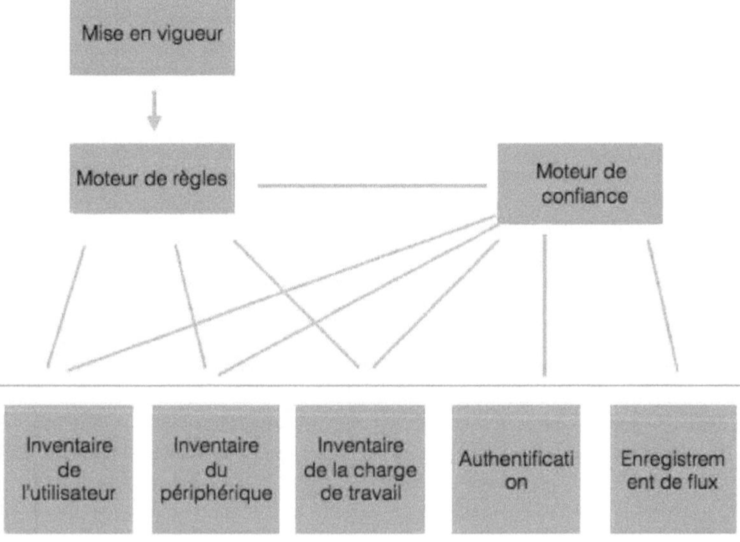

Figure 4-4

In an inventory, a primary key exists that represents only the entity being tracked. In the case of a user, the likely choice is the username; for a device, it may be a serial number. When a zero trust agent undergoes authentication, it authenticates its identity against this primary key in the inventory. Think of it this way: a user authenticates against a given username. The rules engine knows the username and whether the user has been successfully authenticated. The username is then used as the primary key for searching the user's inventory.

Keeping this flow and purpose in mind will help you choose the right primary keys, depending on your implementation and authentication choices.

A historical data store is a little different. Historical data stores are primarily kept for risk analysis purposes. They are useful for examining recent/past behaviors and patterns to assess risk in relation to a particular request or action. Trust engine components are most likely to consume this data, as trust/risk determinations are the primary responsibility of the engine.

One can imagine many types of historical data stores, and when it comes to risk analysis, the sky is the limit. Some common examples include user accounting records and flow data. Regardless of the data stored, it must be searchable using the primary key of one of the inventory systems.

We will discuss various inventory stores and historical data as we introduce related concepts throughout this book.

Summary

This chapter has focused on the systems responsible for making the final decision on whether to allow a particular request in a zero-trust network. This decision is an essential component of such a network, and therefore must be carefully designed and isolated to ensure its reliability.

We have divided this responsibility into four key systems: the application, the policy engine, the trust engine and the data stores. These components are logical areas of responsibility. While they could be collapsed into fewer physical systems, the author prefers an isolated design.

The runtime system is responsible for ensuring that the policy engine's authorization decision takes effect. This system, being in the data path of the user traffic, is best implemented in a way where the policy decision is referenced and then applied. Depending on the architecture chosen, the policy engine may be notified before a request occurs, or during the processing of that same request.

The policy engine is the key system that calculates the authorization decision based on the data available to it and the policy definitions that have been created by the system administrators. This system should be highly isolated. The defined policy should ideally be stored separately from the engine and should use good software development practices to ensure that changes are understood, reviewed and not lost as the policy moves from proposal to implementation. In addition, because zero-trust networks expect to have a much more refined policy, mature organizations choose to distribute the responsibility for defining this policy across the organization with the security teams reviewing proposed changes.

The trust engine is a new concept in security systems. This engine is responsible for calculating a trust score for system components using static and inferred algorithms derived from past behavior. The trust score is a numerical determination of the trustworthiness of a component and allows policy writers to focus on the level of trust required to access certain resources rather than the specific details of actions that may reduce that trust.

The final element of this part of the system is the authoritative data sources that capture current and historical data that can be used to make the authorization decision. These data stores should focus on being sources of truth. The rules engine, trust engine, and perhaps third-party systems can leverage this data, so collecting this data will have a decent return on investment from capturing it.

The next chapter will explore how devices gain and maintain trust.

Chapter 5:

Confidence-building measures

Device trust in a zero-trust network is extremely critical. It is also an extremely difficult problem. The device is the battleground on which security is won or lost. Most compromises involve a malicious actor gaining access to a trusted device; and once that access is gained, the device cannot be trusted to attest to its own security.

This chapter discusses the many systems and processes that must be in place to have sufficient trust of the devices deployed on the network. We will focus on the role that each of these systems plays in the larger goal of truly trusting a device. Each technology is complicated in itself. While we can't go into exhaustive detail about each protocol or system, we will try to provide enough detail to help you understand the technology and avoid potential pitfalls when using it.

We start by learning how devices earn their trust in the first place.

Start the trust

When a new device arrives, it is usually given a level of trust equal to that of the manufacturer and distributor. For most people, this is a fairly high level of trust (justified or not). However, this inherited trust only exists in Meatspace, and it is necessary to inject this trust into the device itself.

There are several ways to inject (and maintain) this trust in hardware. Of course, the device ecosystem is huge and the exact approach will differ on a case-by-case basis, but some basic principles apply across the board. These principles reduce most differences to implementation details.

The first of these principles has been known for a long time: golden images. No matter how you get your devices, you should always load a good image. The software can be difficult to verify; rather than doing it several times hastily (or not at all), it makes sense to do it once and certify an image for distribution.

Loading a "clean" image onto a device gives it great confidence. You can be reasonably sure that the software running on it is validated by you and secure. For this reason, recording the last thumbnail of a device that was imaged is an excellent way to determine how much trust it gets on the network.

Safe start-up

There are of course ways to subvert devices so that they retain the implant through reimaging and other low-level operations, because in these cases the implant is usually quite low-level.

Secure boot is one way to help combat this type of attack. This involves loading a public key into the device firmware, which is used to validate the driver and operating system loader signatures to ensure that nothing has been slipped in between. While effective, support is limited to certain devices and operating systems. More on this later.

Being able to certify the software running on a device is only the first step. The device must still be able to identify itself to the resources it is trying to access. This is usually done by generating a unique device certificate that is signed by your private certificate authority. When communicating with network resources, the device presents its signed certificate. This certificate not only proves that it is a known device, but also provides a method of identification. Using the details embedded in the certificate, the device can be associated with data from the device inventory, which can be used to make further decisions.

Generate and secure identity

In providing a signed certificate by which a device can be identified, it is necessary to store the associated private key in a secure manner. This is not an easy task. Theft of the private key would allow an attacker to impersonate a trusted device. This is the worst possible scenario for device authentication.

A simple but insecure way to do this is to configure the access rights to the key so that only the most privileged user (root or administrator) can access it. This is the least desirable storage method, as an attacker who gains high access can exfiltrate the unprotected key.

Another method is to encrypt the private key. This is better than relying on simple permissions, although it does pose usability issues because a password (or other secret material) must be provided to decrypt and use the key. This may not be a problem for an end-user device, as the user can be prompted to enter the password, although this is generally not possible for server deployments; human interaction is required for each software restart.

The best way to store device keys is through secure cryptoprocessors. These devices, commonly referred to as hardware security modules (HSMs) or secure platform modules (TPMs), provide a secure area in which cryptographic operations can be performed. They provide a limited API that can be used to generate asymmetric encryption keys, where the private key never leaves the security module. Since even the operating system cannot directly access a private key stored by a security module, they are very difficult to steal.

Identity security in staticand dynamic systems

In relatively static systems, it is common for an operator to be involved when new hosts are provisioned. This makes the injection story easy - the trusted human can directly cut the new keys on behalf of the hosts. Of course, as the infrastructure grows, this overhead will become problematic.

In automating the provisioning and signing process, there is an important decision to be made: should a human be involved when signing new certificates? The answer to that depends largely on your sensibilities.

A signed device certificate is quite powerful and serves to identify anything with a private key as a genuine and trusted device. Just as we take steps to protect their local theft, we must also protect against their frivolous generation. If your installation is particularly sensitive, you may choose to involve a human each time a new certificate is signed.

DigiNotar signature service

In 2011, a company called DigiNotar suffered a security breach. This breach was significant because DigiNotar was a public certificate authority. Attackers were able to compromise the certificate signing infrastructure and used this position to sign certificates of their choosing. It is estimated that over 300,000 users had their personal data exposed by these fraudulent certificates. DigiNotar's certificates were immediately blacklisted by browsers around the world, and the company declared bankruptcy shortly thereafter. This breach underscores the importance of a secure signing infrastructure and process.

If the provisioning is automated, but still human-centric, it makes perfect sense to allow the person conducting that action to also authorize the associated signature request. Having a human involved at all times is the best way to prevent unauthorized requests from being approved. Humans are not perfect however they are susceptible to fatigue and other flaws. For this reason, it is recommended that they be responsible for approving only those requests that they themselves have initiated.

It is possible to accomplish provisioning and signature authorization in a single step by using a one-time password (TOTP). The TOTP can be provided with the provisioning request and passed to the signing service for verification, as shown in Figure 5-1. This simple but powerful mechanism allows human control over the signing of new certificates while imposing minimal administrative overhead. Since a TOTP can only be used once, a TOTP verification failure is an important security event.

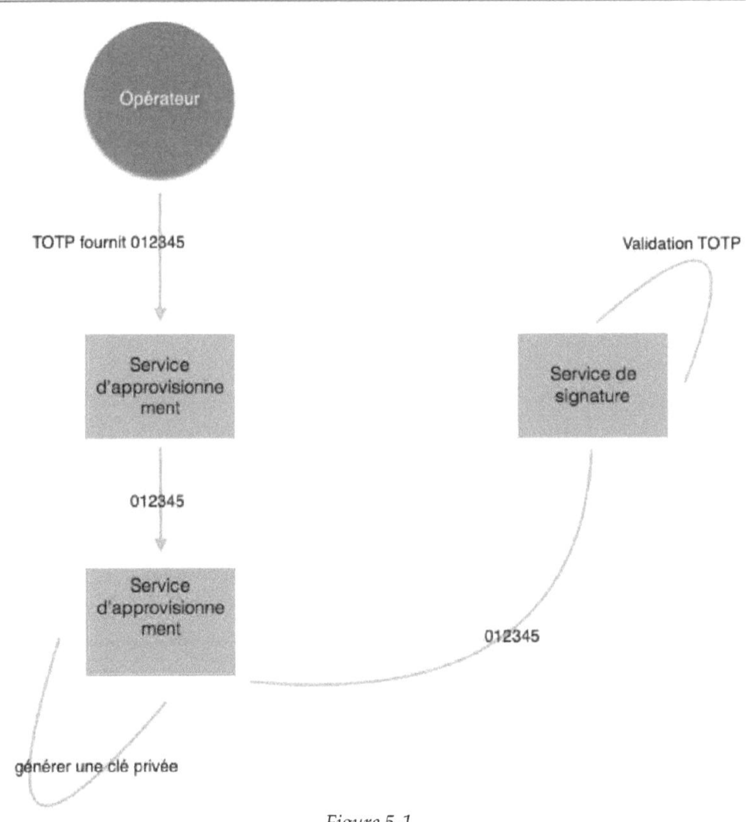

Figure 5-1

Needless to say, none of this applies if you want to fully automate the provisioning of new hosts. Often called "auto-scaling", systems that can grow and shrink themselves are usually found in large, highly automated facilities. Allowing a system to scale itself decreases the amount of care and feeding required, which greatly reduces administrative overhead and costs.

Signing a certificate is a trust-intensive operation; and just as with other zero-trust components, that trust must come from somewhere. There are three common choices:

- a human
- the resource manager
- the image or device

Human is an easy and secure choice for relatively static infrastructure or end-user devices, but obviously not for automated infrastructure. In this case, you have to choose the resource manager or the image ... or both.

Depending on your needs, you may not want to grant this capability entirely to the resource manager. In this case, the credentials can be "baked" into an image. This is generally not advisable as a primary mechanism, as it places too much responsibility on the image store; and protecting and rotating images can be dangerous. Similarly, HSMs or TPMs can be used to provide a hardware-related device certificate. This is better than "baking" material into the image, but asking a TPM-supported device to sign a new certificate is still not ideal, especially when considering cloud deployments.

A good way to mitigate these issues is to require both the resource manager and a trusted image/device. Generic authentication material "baked into" the image (or a registered TPM key) can be used to secure communication with the signing service and can serve as a component in a multi-faceted authorization. Examples of components to consider for authorization include:
- registered TPM key or image key
- correct IP address
- Valid TOTP (generated by the resource manager)
- Expected certificate properties (i.e. expected common name)

By validating all of these points, the certificate signing service can be fairly certain that the request is legitimate. The resource manager alone cannot request a certificate, and since it does not have access to the hosts, it can only do so much. Similarly, a stolen image alone cannot request a certificate, as it asks the resource manager to validate that it has provisioned the host and waits for the request.

By dividing these responsibilities and requiring multiple systems to assert validity, we can safely (well, as safely as possible) remove humans from the loop.

Resource managers and containers

Sometimes it comes down to terminology. In host-centric systems, resource managers create self-scaling systems, making decisions about when and where capacity is needed. In contained environments, the same decisions are made and executed by a resource scheduler. For zero-trust applications, these components are virtually identical and the principles apply equally to host-centric and container-centric environments.

Authentication of devices with the control plan

Now that we know how to store identity in a new device or host, we need to determine how to validate that identity over the network. Fortunately, there are a number of open standards and technologies available to accomplish this. Here, we'll discuss two of these technologies and why they're so important for device authentication: first we'll learn about X.509 before moving on to TPM.

These technologies benefit from widespread deployment and support, although this is not always the case. While we discuss realistic approaches to securing legacy devices in Chapter 8, we will further explore here what the future might hold for zero-trust support in legacy hardware.

X.509

X.509 is perhaps the most important standard for device identity and authentication. It defines the format of public key certificates, revocation lists, and methods used to validate certification chains. The framework it puts forward helps form the identity used for authenticating secure devices in almost all of the protocols we will discuss in this book.

One of the most interesting things about X.509 is that the public/private key pairs used to prove identity can also be used to initiate encrypted communication. This is just one of the many reasons why X.509 is so valuable for Internet security.

certificate chains and certification authorities

For a certificate to mean anything, it must be trusted. A certificate can be created by anyone, so having one with the right name doesn't mean much. A trusted party must approve the validity of the certificate by digitally signing it. A certificate without a "real" signature is called a self-signed certificate and is usually only used for testing purposes.

It is the responsibility of the registration authority (a role usually filled by the certification authority) to ensure that the details of the certificate are correct before allowing it to be signed. By signing the certificate, a verifiable code is created from the signed certificate to the parent. If the signed certificate has the right properties, it can sign other certificates, resulting in a chain. The certification authority is at the root of this chain.

By trusting a certificate authority (CA), you are trusting the validity of all the certificates signed by it. This is very convenient, because it allows us to distribute only a small number of public keys in advance - the CA's public keys, that is. All certificates provided from there can be linked to the known CA and therefore trusted. We discussed the concept of the CA and PKI in general more in Chapter 2.

Device identity and X.509

The primary capability of an X.509 certificate is to prove identity. It uses two keys instead of one: a public key and a private key. The public key is distributed and the private key is held by the certificate owner. The owner can prove the presence of the private key by encrypting a small piece of data that can only be decrypted by the public key. This is called public key cryptography or asymmetric cryptography.

The X.509 certificate itself contains a wealth of configurable information. It has a set of standard fields, as well as a relatively healthy ecosystem of extensions, which allow it to carry metadata that can be used for authorization purposes. Here is a small sample of typical

```
Certificate:
    Data:
        Version: 3 (0x2)
        Serial Number:
            ea:78:b1:33:90:2e:2b:a0
        Signature Algorithm: sha1WithRSAEncryption
        Issuer: C=US, ST=California, L=San Francisco,

                O=production, OU=web, CN=web01.example.com
        Validity
            Not Before: Oct 27 23:33:33 2016 GMT
            Not After : Oct 27 23:33:33 2017 GMT
        Subject: C=US, ST=California, L=San Francisco,
                O=production, OU=web, CN=web01.example.com
        Subject Public Key Info:
            Public Key Algorithm: rsaEncryption
            RSA Public Key: (512 bit)
                Modulus (512 bit):
                    00:d1:e2:54:b1:26:b1:49:64:72:6d:eb:54:fe:0a:
                    fc:74:56:a8:86:f2:54:32:7e:09:fa:06:ae:94:2b:
                    de:a5:9d:3b:9d:c3:d9:ad:08:3b:ed:b8:96:a7:0d:
                    2f:65:61:49:7f:f0:b0:85:95:af:39:e2:64:82:4c:
                    ff:97:76:12:6b
                Exponent: 65537 (0x10001)
        X509v3 extensions:
            X509v3 Subject Key Identifier:
                DD:92:3E:9E:A8:28:F0:85:FC:A6:4D:C1:1A:2A:BE:35:2D:F7:7A:55
            X509v3 Authority Key Identifier:

 keyid:DD:92:3E:9E:A8:28:F0:85:FC:A6:4D:C1:1A:2A:BE:35:2D:F7:7A:55
                DirName:/C=US/ST=California/L=San
Francisco/O=production/OU=web ...
```



```
                serial:EA:78:B1:33:90:2E:2B:A0


            X509v3 Basic Constraints:
                CA:TRUE
    Signature Algorithm: sha1WithRSAEncryption
        33:41:f4:22:72:aa:7b:e9:d2:07:a0:e7:aa:5d:21:89:66:84:
        8e:11:87:8f:1b:c1:b8:dd:6b:76:6d:24:55:eb:20:61:6d:89:
        15:90:78:8c:81:e1:48:e4:45:3d:fe:0e:fd:92:78:84:2c:bc:
        0c:6e:06:03:80:95:5f:5d:1b:41
```

One of the fields in the code snippet is called the Subject field. The subject field stores information about the owner, which in our case is a device (or host). Traditionally, fields such as Organization (O) and Organizational Unit (OU) are exactly as they sound; but in data center applications, they can be reused to provide a richer identity.

The example shows one approach, where O is mapped to the environment and OR is mapped to the host role. Since the certificate is signed and trusted, we can use this information to make authorization decisions. Using X.509 fields in this way means that access to the device can be granted without calling an external service, as long as the server knows who/what to expect.

Public and private components

As mentioned earlier, X.509 deals with key pairs rather than a single key. While it is very common for these to be RSA key pairs, they do not have to be. X.509 supports many types of key pairs, and we have recently begun to see the popularization of other key types (such as ECDSA)

Private key storage

X.509 is incredibly useful for device authentication, but it doesn't solve all the problems. It still has a private key, and that private key must be protected. If the private key is compromised, the identity and privacy of the device will also be vulnerable. While other zero-trust measures help guard against the damage this could cause (such as user/application authentication or authorization risk analysis), this is considered the worst case and should be avoided at all costs.

Private keys can be encrypted when stored, requiring a password to decrypt. This is good practice as it would require more than just disk access to successfully steal, but is only practical for user facing devices. In the data center, private key encryption doesn't solve the problem because you still have to store the password or transmit it to the server, so much so that the password becomes as cumbersome as the private key itself. Hardware security modules (HSMs) go a long way in trying to protect the private key.

They contain hardware that can generate a public/private key pair and store the private key in secure memory. It is not possible to read the private key from the HSM. It is only possible to ask the HSM to perform an operation with it on your behalf. This way, the private key cannot be stolen because it is protected in the hardware. We will talk more about TPM, a type of HSM, in the next section.

X.509 for device authentication

The application of X.509 to device authentication in a zero-trust network is immense. It is a cornerstone of proof of device identity for just about every protocol we have and is essential to enable end-to-end encryption. Every device in a Zero Trust network must have an X.509 certificate.

However, there is an important consideration to make. We use X.509 to authenticate a device, but the heart of the whole system - the private key - is decidedly software. If the private key is stolen, the entire authentication of the device is a sham!

These certificates are often used as a proxy for actual device authentication because the keys are so long and cumbersome that you never write one down or remember any of them. They are something that would be downloaded and installed, and because of that, they don't tend to track users - they more generally track devices.

While the risk associated with the private key problem can be determined to be acceptable, it remains a serious problem, especially for zero trust. Fortunately, we can see some paths forward, and by leveraging MPTs, it is possible to inextricably associate a private key with its hardware.

TPMs

A secure platform module (TPM) is a special chip embedded in a computing device. Called a cryptoprocessor, these chips are dedicated to performing cryptographic operations reliably and securely. They include their own firmware and are often considered a computer on a chip.

This design allows for a small and simple hardware API that can be easily verified and analyzed for vulnerability. By providing functionality for cryptographic operations, and excluding interfaces to retrieve private keys, we get the security we need without ever exposing secret keys to the operating system. Instead, they are tied to the hardware.

This is a very important property and the reason why TPMs are so important for device authentication in Zero Trust networks. The big software frameworks for identity and authentication (like X.509) do a lot for device authentication. But without a way to bind the software key to the hardware device it is trying to identify, we can't really call it device identity. TPMs solve this problem by providing the necessary binding.

Data encryption using a TPM

TPM modules generate and store what is called a storage root key or SRK. This key pair represents the root of trust for the TPM device. Data encrypted with its public key can only be decrypted by the original TPM.

The astute reader might question the usefulness of this feature in the application of bulk data encryption. We know that asymmetric cryptographic operations are very expensive and therefore not suitable for encrypting relatively large data. Thus, in order to take advantage of TPM for bulk data encryption, we need to reduce the amount of data that SRK is responsible for securing.

An easy way to do this is to generate a random encryption key, encrypt the global data using known symmetric encryption (i.e., AES), and then use the SRK to encrypt the resulting AES key. This strategy, shown in Figure 5-2, ensures that the encryption key cannot be recovered except in the presence of the TPM that originally protected it.

Most TPM libraries available for open consumption perform these steps for you, through the use of helper methods. It is recommended that you inspect the inner workings of these methods before using them.

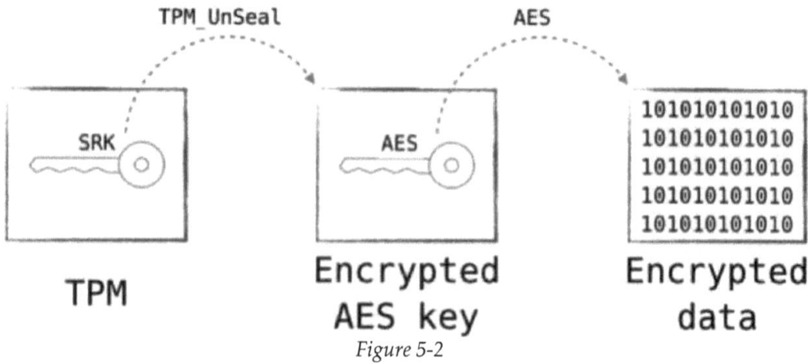

Figure 5-2

Many TPM libraries (such as TrouSerS) create intermediate keys when encrypting data using TPM. In other words, they tell the TPM to create a new asymmetric key pair, use the public key to encrypt the AES key, and finally use the SRK key to encrypt the private key. When decrypting the data, you must first decrypt the intermediate private key, use it to decrypt the AES key, and then decrypt the original data.

This implementation seems strange, but there are some relatively sound reasons for it. One reason is that the extra level of indirection allows greater flexibility in the distribution of secure data. Both SRK and intermediate keys support passwords, so the use of an intermediate key allows for the use of an additional, perhaps more familiar secret phrase.

This may or may not make sense for your particular deployment. For the purposes of "This key should only be decryptable on this device", it is OK (and more efficient) to bypass the use of an intermediate key, if you wish.

The most important application of TPM-supported secure storage is to protect the device's X.509 private key. This secret key is used to prove the identity of the device, and if stolen, the identity. Encrypting the private key using TPM means that while the key can still be retrieved from the drive, it will not be recoverable without the original hardware.

Key theft is always possible

Encrypting the device's private key and wrapping the key with SRK does not solve all theft vectors. It protects the key from being read directly from disk, although an attacker with elevated privileges may still be able to read it from memory or simply have the TPM perform the operation for them.

The following two sections provide additional information on how to further validate the identity of the material (beyond the X.509 identity).

Platform configuration registers

Platform configuration registers (PCRs) are an important TPM feature. They provide storage locations in which the hashes of the running software are stored. It starts with the BIOS hash, then the boot record, its configuration, etc. This sequence of hashes can then be used to attest that the system is in a configuration or state

```
PCR-03: B2 A8 3B 0E BF 2F ...          # Option ROM Configuration
PCR-04: 78 93 CF 58 0E E1 ...          # MBR
PCR-05: 72 A7 A9 6C 96 39 ...          # MBR Configuration
```

approved. Here is a truncated example of the first registers stored in the TPM:

```
PCR-00: A8 5A 84 B7 38 FC ...          # BIOS
PCR-01: 11 40 C1 7D 0D 25 ...          # BIOS Configuration
PCR-02: A3 82 9A 64 61 85 ...          # Option ROM
```

This is useful in several ways, including ensuring that only authorized software configurations are allowed to decrypt data. This can be done by transmitting a set of known PCR values using the TPM to encrypt certain data. This is known as "sealing" the data. Sealed data can only be decrypted by the TPM that sealed it, and only when the PCR values match.

Since PCR values cannot be changed or overridden, we can use TPM sealing to ensure that our secret data is not only locked to the device, but also locked to a specific configuration and software version. This helps prevent hackers from using access to the device to obtain the private key, since only unmodified and approved software can unlock it.

Remote certification

We have learned many ways that we can use embedded device security to protect private keys and other sensitive device data. The unfortunate truth is that as long as a private key is stored outside of a physical TPM, it is still vulnerable to theft. This fact remains because all it takes to recover the private key is to convince the TPM to unlock it once. This action reveals the actual private key - something that is not possible when it is stored on the TPM.

Fortunately, the TPM allows us to uniquely identify it. This is another key pair called an endorsement key (EK), and each TPM has a unique one. The private component of an EK exists only on the TPM itself and thus remains completely inaccessible by the operating system.

Remote attestation is a method by which the TPM generates something called a "quote", which is then transmitted securely to a remote party. The quote includes a list of current PCR values, signed using the EK. A remote party can use this to assert both the identity of the host (since the EK is unique to the TPM) and the state/configuration of the software (since the PCRs cannot be changed). We'll talk more about how the quote can be transmitted in Chapter 8.

Why not just TPM?

You might ask: why not use TPM exclusively for device identification and authentication, and why include X.509?

Currently, the TPM access is cumbersome and non-performing. It can provide a certificate X.509 to attest its identity, but it is limited in its interaction with the private key. For example, the key used for attestation is only capable of signing data from the TPM. For a protocol like TLS, this is a deal-breaker.

There have been some attempts to force TPM attestation protocols into a more flexible form (such as the IETF-latze-tls-tpm-extns-02 draft, which defines a TLS extension for device authentication via TPM).

There are a few open source implementations of remote attestation, including one in the popular IKE strongSwan daemon. This opens the door to using TPM data to not only authenticate an IPsec connection, but also authorize it using PCR data to validate that the host is running genuine, unmodified software.

TPM for device authentication

It is clear that TPMs are the best option for strong device authentication in mature Zero-Trust networks. They are the linchpin between the software identity and the physical hardware. However, there are some limitations.

Many data center workloads are heterogeneous and isolated, such as virtual machines or containers, both of which need to use TPM virtualization to enable the isolated workload to achieve similar goals. While there are implementations available (such as vTPM for Xen), approval must still be anchored in a hardware TPM, and designing a secure TPM system that can migrate live is difficult.

Furthermore, TPM support is still rare despite its many uses and strengths. While the use of TPM is expected in the context of device authentication in mature Zero-Trust networks, it should not be considered a requirement. Adopting TPM support is no small feat, and there is much less fruit in terms of adoption and zero-trust migration.

Hardware for Zero Trust

The most common approach to supporting legacy devices in a Zero Trust network is to use an authentication proxy. The authentication proxy terminates the zero trust relationship and forwards the connection to the legacy host.

While it is possible to enforce a policy between the authentication proxy and the legacy backend, this is far from ideal and shares a handful of attack vectors with traditional perimeter networks. When dealing with legacy devices, it is best to place the Zero Trust endpoint as close to the device as possible.

At the time of writing, an authentication proxy is probably the best and most reasonable option, although it seems there is room for a dedicated hardware device. This device can act as a zero-trust client, carrying a TPM chip and plugging directly into the Ethernet port of an older device. Pairing the two in your inventory management system can allow seamless integration between existing devices and a zero-trust network.

There are many applications that would benefit greatly from such a device. SCADA and HVAC systems, for example, come to mind. While such a device is admittedly purely a fantasy at the moment, it remains an interesting thought experiment.

Inventory management

Authenticating the identity and integrity of a device provides high zero-trust security, but being able to identify a device as belonging to the organization is only part of the challenge. There is a lot of other information we need to calculate policy and make enforcement decisions.

Inventory management involves cataloging devices and their properties. Maintaining these records is equally important for servers and client machines. It is sometimes more useful to think of these entities as network entities rather than physical entities. Although they are in fact physical devices, they can also be logical entities on the network.

For example, it is conceivable that a virtual machine or container could be considered a "device", depending on your needs. They have many of the same descriptive properties that a real server might have, after all. Forwarding all virtual machine traffic from a single host to a policy takes us right back to the perimeter model. Instead, the zero-trust model advocates that workloads be tracked to direct the network policies they need. This inventory (or workload) database can in this case be specialized to accommodate the high rates of change that virtualized/containerized environments experience. Thus, while the traditional inventory management system and the workload scheduler may be different systems, they can still work together; For the purposes of this book, the scheduler service can act as an inventory management system, as shown in Figure 5-3.

It is not uncommon to have more than one inventory management system. As an example, many companies have both asset management and configuration management software. Both of these store device metadata that is useful to us; they just store different sets, collected in different ways.

Configuration management as an inventory database

Many configuration management systems, such as Chef or Puppet, offer modes in which data about the nodes they run is held in a centralized database. Name, IP address, and server "type" are examples of the type of information typically found in a CM-supported database. Using configuration management in this way is an easy first step towards developing an inventory database if you don't already have one.

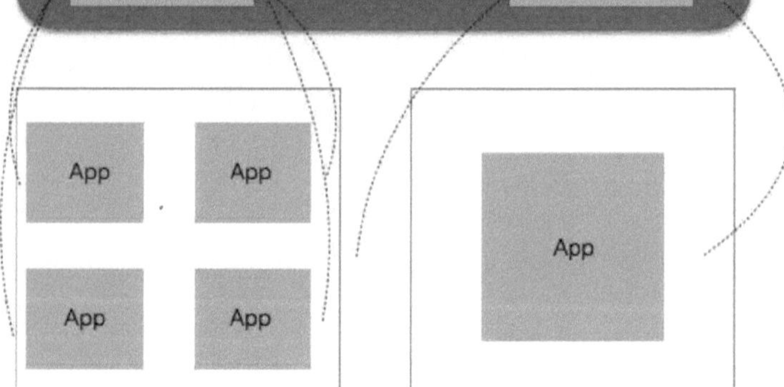

Figure 5-3

Know what to expect

One of the great powers of a zero trust network is that it knows what to expect. Trusted entities can introduce expectations into the system, allowing all levels of access to be denied by default - only expected actions / requests are allowed.

An inventory database is a major component in achieving this capability. A huge amount of information about what to expect can be generated from this data; things like what user or application should be running, what locations we might expect, or even what type of operating system are all pieces of information that can be used to set expectations.

In the data center, these expectations can be very high. For example, when provisioning a new server, we often know what IP address it will be assigned and what it will be used for. We can use this information to drive network ACLs and/or host-based firewalls, poking holes in that specific IP address only when necessary. This way we can deny all traffic, allowing only the very specific flows we expect. The more properties we expect, the better.

However, this is not an easy prospect for customer-oriented systems. Clients operate in new and unexpected ways all the time, and know exactly what to expect from them and when it is very difficult. Data center servers often have relatively static and long-lived connections to a well-defined set of hosts or services. In contrast, clients tend to make many short-lived connections to a variety of services, the timing, frequency, and patterns of which can vary organically.

In order to accommodate the wild nature of client-oriented systems, we need a slightly different approach. One way is to simply allow global access to the service and protect it with mutually authenticated TLS, which requires the client to provide a device certificate before it can be communicated with. The device certificate can be used to look up the device in the inventory database and determine whether or not it should be authorized. The advantage is that many systems already support the mutually authenticated TLS protocol and specialized client software is not strictly required. Reasonably strong security can be provided without compromising accessibility or ease of use.

However, a major drawback of this approach is that the service is globally accessible. Requiring client certificates is an excellent way to mitigate this danger. However, we have seen from vulnerabilities like Heartbleed that the attack surface of a TLS server is relatively large. Furthermore, the existence of resources can be discovered simply by scanning them, as we can talk TCP to the resource before authenticating with it.

How can we ensure that we don't hire unreliable clients? There must be some untrusted communication, after all. What comes before authentication?

Secure introduction

The very first connection of a new device is precarious. After all, these packets must be admitted somewhere, and if they are not strongly authenticated, there is a risk. Therefore, the first system contacted by a new device requires a mechanism to authenticate that initial contact.

This arrangement is commonly referred to as secure introduction. It is the process by which a new entity is introduced into an existing entity in such a way that trust is transferred to it. There are several ways to do this; the method by which an operator passes a TOTP code to a provider in order to authorize a certificate request is a form of secure introduction.

The best (and perhaps only) way to do a secure introduction is to establish an expectation. Secure introduction almost always involves a trusted third party. This is a system that has already been introduced, and it has the ability to introduce new systems. This trusted third party is the system that then coordinates/validates the specifics of the system to be introduced and sets the appropriate expectations.

Secure entry for client systems

The secure introduction of customer-facing systems can be difficult due to the hard-to-predict nature of wild customers. When public exposure of a client touchpoint is considered too risky, it is necessary to turn to more complex systems. The currently accepted approach is to use a form of signaling called pre-authentication, which announces a customer's intentions just before acting. We'll talk more about pre-authentication in Chapter 8.

What makes a good secure entry system?

Single use
The credentials and privileges associated with the introduction must be one-time use, preventing an attacker from compromising and reusing the key.

Short term
The credentials and privileges associated with the introduction must be short-lived, preventing the accumulation of valid but unused keys.

Third party
Leveraging a third party for introduction allows for segregation of duties, prevents the introduction of poor security practices, and mitigates operational headaches.

While these requirements may at first seem stringent, they can be met in fairly simple ways. A good example can be found in the way the Chef software implements host introduction. Originally, there was a single secret (considered the "validation certificate") that was qualified to admit any host that possessed it as a new node. Thus, introduction would involve copying this secret to the target machine (or "baking" it into the image), using it to register the new node, and then deleting it.

This approach is neither single-use nor short-lived. If the secret is recovered, it could be used by a malicious actor to direct application traffic to hosts controlled by the attacker, or even cause a denial of service.

Modern Chef takes a new approach. Instead of having a static validation certificate, the provisioning system (via the Chef "knife" client utility) communicates with the Chef server and creates a new client and an associated client certificate.
It then creates the new host and transmits its client certificate. In this way, an expectation for the new client has been set. Although these credentials are not short-lived, they remain as a superior approach.

Renewed confidence in the device

It is important to accept that no level of security is perfect - not even your own. Once we recognize this fact, we can begin to mitigate its consequences. The natural progression is that the longer a device operates, the more likely it is to be compromised. That's why the age of the device is a heavily weighted confidence signal.

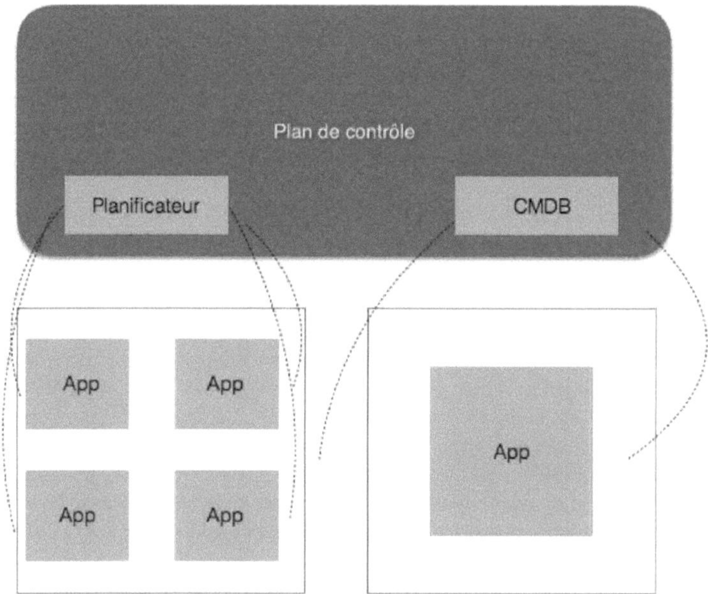

Figure 5-4

For this reason, rotation is very important. We've talked at length about the importance of rotation, and devices are no different. Of course, this "spin" manifests itself in different ways depending on your definition of "device". If your infrastructure is running in a cloud, perhaps a "device" is a host instance. In that case, rotation is easy: just unmount the instance and create a new one (you're using configuration management, right?). If you're using physical hardware, however, this prospect is a bit more difficult.

Reimaging is a good way to rotate a device in a logical way. It's a low-level operation that will successfully remove the majority of persistent threats we see in the wild today. A freshly reimaged device can be trusted more than one that has been running for a year. While reimaging does not address hardware or other low-level attacks such as those shown in Figure 5-4, it is a reasonable compromise in places where physical rotation is more difficult. The data center and supply chain security partially mitigate this problem.

When it comes to managing client devices, the story changes a bit. Re-imaging a client device is extremely annoying to users. They personalize the device (and its contents) over time in ways that are difficult to preserve effectively or securely. Often, when they receive a new device, they want to transfer the old image! This is not good news for people trying to secure client devices.

The solution depends largely on your use case. The trade-off between security and convenience will be very clear in this area. Everyone agrees that client devices should be rotated and/or reimagined from time to time, but it's up to you how often. There is an important relationship to keep in mind: the less a device is rotated or reimaged, the more stringent your endpoint security should be.

Without the relatively strong guarantees of device security that we get with rotation, we have to look for other methods to renew confidence in a long-running device. There are two general methods by which this can be done: local measurement or remote measurement.

Local measure

Local measurement can be of two types: hardware or software supported. Hardware supported measurement is more secure and reliable, but limited in capacity. Software supported measurement is much less safe and reliable, but practically unlimited in its measurement capabilities.

A good option for local hardware-based measurement is to leverage the TPM for remote attestation. Remote attestation uses a hardware device to provide a signed response describing the hashes of software running on that machine. The response is very reliable and very difficult to reproduce.

However, it usually only gives an image of the low-level or specifically targeted software. If an attacker has managed to run an unauthorized process in user space, the TPM will not be very useful in detecting it; thus, it has limited capability. See "Remote Attestation" for more information.

Software-supported local measurement involves some sort of agent installed on the endpoint that is used to report health and status measurements. This may be a managed antivirus client or policy enforcement agents. These agents go to great lengths to attest and prove the validity of the metrics they report, but even cursory thought quickly leads to the conclusion that these efforts are usually futile. Software-backed metrics lack the protection provided by hardware metrics, and an attacker with sufficient privileges can subvert systems like this.

Remote measurement

Remote measurement is the better of the two options for one simple reason: it benefits from separation of duties. A compromised host can report anything it wants, possibly distorting the information to hide the attacker. This is not possible with remote or passive measurement, as a completely different system determines the health of the host in question.

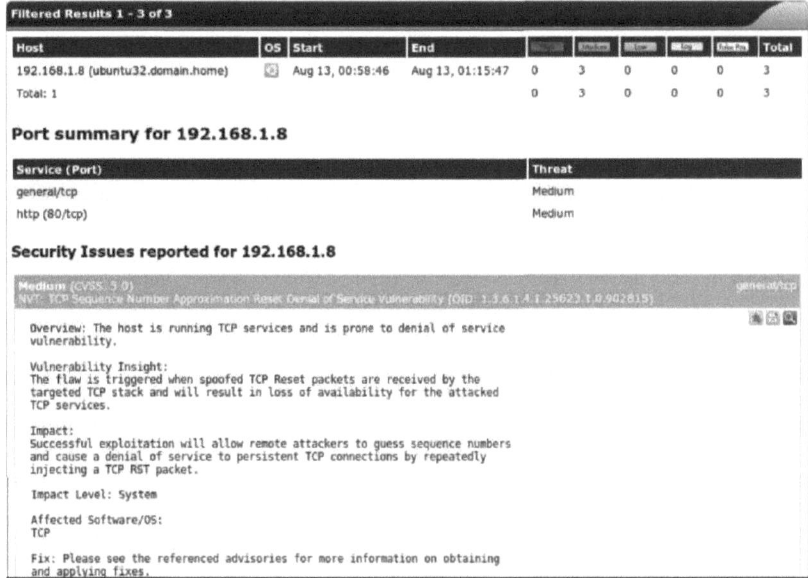

Figure 5-5

Traditionally, the remote measurement is performed as a simple vulnerability scan. The system in question will be periodically probed by a scanning device, which observes the response. The response provides some information, such as the operating system running on that device, the services that may be active on it, and perhaps even the version of those services.

The results of the scan can be cross-referenced with known signatures, such as malware or vulnerable versions of legitimate software, producing a report similar to that shown in Figure 5-5. The detection of known-bad signatures can then influence the trustworthiness of the device in an appropriate manner.

There are a number of open source and commercial options available in the area of vulnerability scanning, including OpenVAS, Nessus and Metasploit. These projects are all fairly mature and supported by many organizations.

Unfortunately, vulnerability scanning has the same fundamental problem as local measurement: it relies on interrogating the endpoint. It's the difference between asking someone if they robbed a bank and watching them rob a bank. Sure, sometimes you can get the robber to admit that they did it, but a professional would never fall for it. Catching them in the act is much more effective. See "Network Communication" for more information on how to solve this dilemma.

Software configuration management

Configuration management is the process of rigorous control and documentation of all software changes. Desired configurations are usually defined as code or data, and checked into a revision control system, which allows changes to be audited, rolled back, etc. There are many commercial and open source options available, the most popular of which are Chef, Puppet, Ansible and CFEngine.

Configuration management software is useful in both data center and client deployments and simply becomes necessary beyond a certain scale. Using such software comes with many security gains, such as the ability to quickly update packages after vulnerability announcements or to similarly assert that there are no vulnerable packages in the wild.

Beyond auditing and strict change control, configuration management can also be used as an agent for dynamic policy configuration. If a node can get a reliable view of the world (or part of it, at least), it can use it to compute the policy and install it locally. However, this functionality is pretty much limited to the data center, because even though dynamic systems hosted on a data center are decidedly more static and predictable than client systems. We'll talk more about this zero-trust mode of operation later.

Inventory based on CM

We've mentioned several times the idea of using a configuration management database for inventory management purposes. This is a great first step towards a mature inventory management system and can provide a rich source of information about the various hosts and software running in your infrastructure.

We like to think of CM (configuration management) based inventory management as an "extra" in that configuration management is

```
languages:
  c:
    gcc:
      description: gcc version 4.8.4 (Ubuntu 4.8.4-
2ubuntu1-14.04)
      version:      4.8.4
  java:
    hotspot:
      build: 24.71-b01, mixed mode
      name:  Java HotSpot(TM) 64-Bit Server VM
    runtime:


      build: 1.7.0_71-b14
      name:  Java(TM) SE Runtime Environment
      version: 1.7.0_71
    perl:
  ... <SNIP> ...
  dmi:
    bios:
      address:        0xE8000
```

```
      all_records:
        Address:                      0xE8000
        BIOS Revision:                4.2
        ROM Size:                     64 kB
        Release Date:                 12/03/2014
        Runtime Size:                 96 kB
        Vendor:                       Xen
        Version:                      4.2.amazon
        application_identifier: BIOS Information
    chassis:
      all_records:
        Asset Tag:                    Not Specified
        Boot-up State:                Safe
```

generally used for all the other benefits it brings. Using it

```
... <SNIP> ...
fqdn:              foo.bar
hostname:          foo
idletime:          2 days 09 hours 48 minutes 37 seconds
idletime_seconds:  208117
init_package:      init
ipaddress:         192.168.1.1
kernel:
  machine: x86_64
  modules:
    ablk_helper:
      refcount: 6
      size:        13597
... <SNIP> ...
network:
  default_gateway:   192.168.1.254
  default_interface: eth0
  interfaces:
    eth0:
      addresses:
        192.168.1.1:
```

as an inventory database is most often for convenience.

Maintaining this view is important: configuration management systems are not designed to function as inventory management systems ... they are designed to act as configuration management systems! Using it as such will surely bring some rough edges, and you will eventually outgrow it. That's not to say you shouldn't do it. It's better to achieve a zero-trust network by making the most of existing technology than to never get there because of the high barrier to entry.

Once we accept this fact, we can begin to exploit the wealth of data provided by CM agents. Using Chef, for example, we can calculate the trust score and write policy on over 1,500 host attributes. Here are a few small snippets illustrating the type of information that the Chef agent collects and stores:

```
            broadcast: 192.168.1.255
            family:    inet
            netmask:   255.255.255.0
            prefixlen: 24
            scope:     Global
        22:00:0A:1E:55:AD:
            family: lladdr
    arp:
        192.168.1.2:   fe:ff:ff:ff:ff:ff
        192.168.1.3:   fe:ff:ff:ff:ff:ff
        192.168.1.254: fe:ff:ff:ff:ff:ff
    encapsulation: Ethernet
```

Searchable inventory

Some CM systems store centrally the data generated by their agents. Typically, this data store is searchable, which opens up many possibilities for young zero-trust networks. For example, the agent can perform a search to retrieve the IP address of all the Web servers in data center A and use the results to configure a host-based firewall.

Some CM systems store centrally the data generated by their agents. Typically, this data store is searchable, which opens up many possibilities for young zero-trust networks. For example, the agent can perform a search to retrieve the IP address of all the Web servers in data center A and use the results to configure a host-based firewall.

Secure source of truth

An important thing to remember when using CM systems in the zero-trust control scheme is that the vast majority of data available to CM systems is self-reported. This is critical to understand, as a compromised machine could potentially become distorted. This can lead to a complete compromise of the zero trust network if these facts are not taken into account in its design.

Thinking back to trust management, the trust system in this case is the provider. Whether it is a human system or an automated system, it is in the best position to assert the critical aspects of a device, including:
- device type
- role
- IP address (in datacenters systems)
- public key

These attributes are considered critical because they are often used to make authorization or authentication decisions. If an attacker can update the role of a device, for example, they can potentially force the network to expose protected services.

For this reason, restricting write access to these attributes is important. Of course, you can still use self-reported attributes to make decisions, but they should never be taken as fact. It is useful to think of self-reported attributes as clues rather than truth.

Using device data for user authorization

The zero-trust model requires authentication and authorization of both the device and the user or application. Since device authentication usually occurs before user authentication, it must be performed without the information obtained through user authentication. This is not the case for user authentication.

When user authentication occurs, the device authentication has already succeeded and the network knows the identity of the device. This position can be leveraged for all sorts of useful contextual knowledge, allowing us to do much stronger user authentication than was previously possible.

One of the most common searches one might do is to check whether one would expect that user, given the type of device or the location of publication. For example, it is unlikely that an engineer's credentials would be used from a mobile device that has been forwarded to HR. So, while the HR employee can freely access a particular resource using their own credentials, user authentication attempts using other credentials may be blocked.

Another good signal is the frequency of user authentication. If you haven't seen a user log in from one of their devices in over a year, and all of a sudden there's a request for that device providing the user's credentials - well, I think it's fair to be a little skeptical. Could it have been stolen?

Of course, there is also a good chance that the request is legitimate. In a case like this, we lower the trust score to indicate that things are a bit fishy. The lower score can then manifest itself in a number of ways, such as still being trusted enough to read parts of the internal wiki, but not trusted enough to log into the financial systems.

Being able to make such decisions is a big part of the zero-trust architecture and highlights the importance of a robust inventory management database. While inventory management is strictly required for device authentication purposes, the contextual benefit given to user authentication is invaluable.

Confidence signals

This section serves as a reference for various trust signals that are useful in calculating the device trust score and write policy.

Elapsed time since the image

Over time, the likelihood that a device has been compromised increases significantly. Endpoint security practices are designed to reduce the risks associated with long-lived or long-running devices. Yet these practices are far from perfect.

Imaging a device ensures that the contents of the hard drive match a known asset. While it is not effective against some lower-level attacks, it provides a reasonably strong assurance of trust. In the moments immediately following the image restoration, there is tremendous trust in the device, as only the hardware or the restoration system itself could taint the process. Over time, however, this confidence dissipates as the system undergoes prolonged exposure.

Historical access

Device authentication patterns, similar to user authentication patterns, are important for understanding risk and act as a good proxy for behavioral filtering. Devices that have not been seen in a while are more suspicious than those that come and go frequently. Perhaps suspicious is the wrong word, but it is certainly unusual.

The request in question may also be related to a resource, and it is wise to consider the device and the resource together in this context. For example, a device that is several months old requesting access to a new resource is more suspicious than a request to a resource that has been accessed weekly for some time. This means that "first" attempts to access a particular resource will be viewed with more skepticism than subsequent attempts.

Similarly, frequency can be analyzed to understand whether a resource is suspiciously overused. A request from a device that made 100 requests in the last day, but only 104 in the last month, is certainly more suspicious than one with 0 in the last day and 4 in the last month.

Rental

While network location is generally something we aim not to consider for important decisions regarding the zero-trust model, it still provides reliable trust signaling in many cases.

Such a case could be a sudden change of location. Since we are talking about device authentication, we can set reasonable expectations about how the device moves. For example, an attempt to authenticate a device from Europe may be quite suspicious if we authorized the same device in the US office a few hours earlier.

It should be noted that this is a bit slippery when it comes to the zero trust model. Zero-trust aims to eliminate advantageous positions within the network, so using network location to determine access rights can be seen as a bit contradictory.

The author recognizes this and acknowledges that location data can be useful in making licensing decisions. However, it is important that this consideration is not binary. One should look for patterns in locations, and never make an absolute decision based solely on location. For example, a policy that dictates that an application can only be accessed from the desktop is a direct violation of the zero trust model.

Network communication models

For devices connected to operator-owned networks, it is possible to measure communication patterns to develop a standard. Sudden changes in this standard are suspect and may affect the system's confidence in such a device.

Network instrumentation and flow collection can quickly detect intrusions by observing them on the network. Making authorization decisions informed by this detection is very powerful. An example might be to shut down database access to a particular web server because that web server has started making DNS queries for hosting providers on another continent.

The same applies to client devices. Consider a desktop computer that never initiated an SSH connection, but is now frequently used by Internet hosts. It is fair to say that this change in behavior is suspicious and should make the device less reliable than before.

Summary

This chapter has focused on how a system can trust a device. This is a surprisingly difficult problem, so many different technologies and practices must be applied to ensure trust in a device.

We started by looking at how trust is injected into a device by human operators. For relatively static systems, we can have one person involved in providing critical credentials; but for dynamic infrastructure, this process must be delegated. This credential information is extremely valuable, so we discussed how to manage it securely.

Devices must eventually participate in the network, so understanding how they authenticate is important. We have covered several technologies, such as X.509 and TPM, that can be used to authenticate a device on the network. Using these technologies along with expected inventory databases can go a long way in providing the checks and balances that give confidence to devices.

Trust is ephemeral and degrades over time, so we discussed mechanisms for renewing trust. In addition, we have discussed the many signals that can be continually used to assess the trustworthiness of a device over time. Perhaps the most important lesson is that a device starts in a state of trust and only gets worse from there. The rate at which its confidence declines is what we would like to keep an eye on.

The next chapter looks at how we can build trust in the users of the system.

Chapter 6: Trusted users

It is tempting to confuse user trust with device trust. Security-conscious organizations can deploy X. 509 certificates on users' devices to provide stronger credentials than passwords provide. One could argue that the device certificate strongly identifies the user, but does it? How do we know that the intended user is actually at the keyboard? Maybe they left their device unlocked and unattended?

User identity conflicting with device identity also faces problems when users have multiple devices, which is becoming more and more the norm. Credentials must be copied between multiple devices, increasing the risk of exposure. Devices may need different credentials depending on their capabilities.

Zero Trust networks identify and trust users independently of devices. Sometimes a user's identification will use the same technology used to identify devices, but we need to make it clear that these are two separate pieces of identification information.

This chapter will explore what it means to identify a user and store their identity. We will discuss when and how to authenticate users. User trust is often strongest when several people are involved. We will therefore discuss how to build group trust and create a culture of security.

Identity authority

Each user has an identity, which represents how they are known in a larger community. In the case of a networked system, a user's identity is how they are known in that system.

Given the large number of people in the world, identifying a user can be a surprisingly difficult problem. Let's explore two types of identity: - Informal identity - Authoritative identity

Informal identity is how groups self-assemble. Consider a real situation where you meet someone. Based on how they look and act, you can construct an identity for that person. When you meet them later, you can reasonably assume they are the same person based on these physical characteristics. You might even be able to identify them from a distance - for example, by hearing their voice.

Informal identity is used in computer systems. Pseudonymous accounts - accounts that are not associated with one's real name - are common in online communities. While an individual's real identity is not necessarily known in these communities, through repeated interactions, an informal identity is created.

Informal identity operates in small groups, where trust between individuals is high and risks are relatively low. This type of identity has obvious weaknesses when the stakes are higher:

- A fictitious identity can be fabricated.
- One can claim the identity of another person.
- You can create several identities.
- Several people can share the same identity.

When a stronger form of identity is required, an authority must create authoritative identification information for individuals. In the real world, this authority often falls to governments. Government-issued IDs (for example, a driver's license or passport) are distributed to individuals to represent their identity to others. For low-risk situations, these identifiers alone are sufficient proof of identity. However, for higher risk situations, cross-checking the identification information against the government database provides a better guarantee.

Computer systems often require a centralized authority for user identity. As in the real world, users are given credentials (of varying strength) that identify them in the system. Depending on the degree of risk, cross-checking credentials against a centralized database may be desired. We will discuss how these systems should work later.

Credentials can be lost or stolen, so it is important that an identity authority have mechanisms in place to allow individuals to regain control of their identity. In the case of government-issued identification, an individual often must present other identifying information (e.g., a birth certificate or fingerprint) to a government authority in order to be re-enrolled. Similarly, computer systems need mechanisms to allow a user to regain control of his or her identity if identifying information is lost or stolen. These systems often require the presentation of an alternative form of verification, such as a recovery code or an alternative authentication certificate. The choice of hardware required to reaffirm one's identity may have security implications that we discuss later.

Generate identity in a private system

Storing and authenticating user identity is one thing, but how do you generate the identity to begin with? Humans interacting with computer systems need a way to digitally represent their identity, and we seek to tie that digital representation as closely as possible to the real-world human.

The genesis of a digital identity, and its initial matching to a human, is a very sensitive operation. Controls to authenticate the human outside your digital system must be strong to prevent an attacker from impersonating a new employee, for example. Similar controls can also be exercised for account recovery procedures when the user is unable to provide their current credentials.

<u>**Attacking identity recovery systems**</u>

Users sometimes tend to forget authentication elements such as passwords or smart cards. To recover the factor (i.e., reset the password), the user must be authenticated by alternative and sometimes non-traditional means. Attacks on such systems are frequent and successful. For example, in 2012, the Amazon account of a popular journalist was hacked and the attacker was able to retrieve the last four digits of the last credit card used. With this information, the attacker called Apple support and "proved" his identity using the recovered number. Be sure to evaluate these reset processes carefully - "secret" information is often less secret than it seems.

Given the sensitivity of this operation, it's important to have good thought and a strong policy on how it's handled. It's essentially a secure introduction for humans, and the good news is, we know how to do that pretty well!

Government-issued identification

It's probably not surprising that one of the main recommendations for human authentication is the use of government-issued identification. After all, human authentication is precisely what they were designed for in the first place!

In some implementations, it may even be desirable to require multiple forms of identification, raising the bar for potential forgers/imposters. It goes without saying that staff must be properly trained to validate these credentials, lest the controls be easily bypassed.

Nothing beats Meatspace (by analogy with cyberspace)

Despite our best efforts, human-based authentication systems still outperform their digital counterparts. It's always a good idea to bootstrap the new digital identity of a human in person. Email or other "blind" introductions are strongly discouraged.

For example, sending a device configured to trust the user on first use (sometimes called TOFU) is not uncommon. However, this method suffers from a physical weakness since the packet is vulnerable to interception or redirection.

Often, the creation of a digital identity is preceded by a lengthy human process, such as a series of interviews or the completion of a corporate contract. The result is that the individual has already been exposed to already trusted people who have learned some of their qualities along the way. This knowledge can be leveraged for additional human authentication, as shown in Figure 6-1.

For example, a hiring manager is well positioned to escort a new hire to a help desk for human authentication, since the hiring manager is likely already familiar with the individual and can attest to their identity. While this is a strong signal of trust, just like anything else in a zero-trust network, it should not be the only method of authentication.

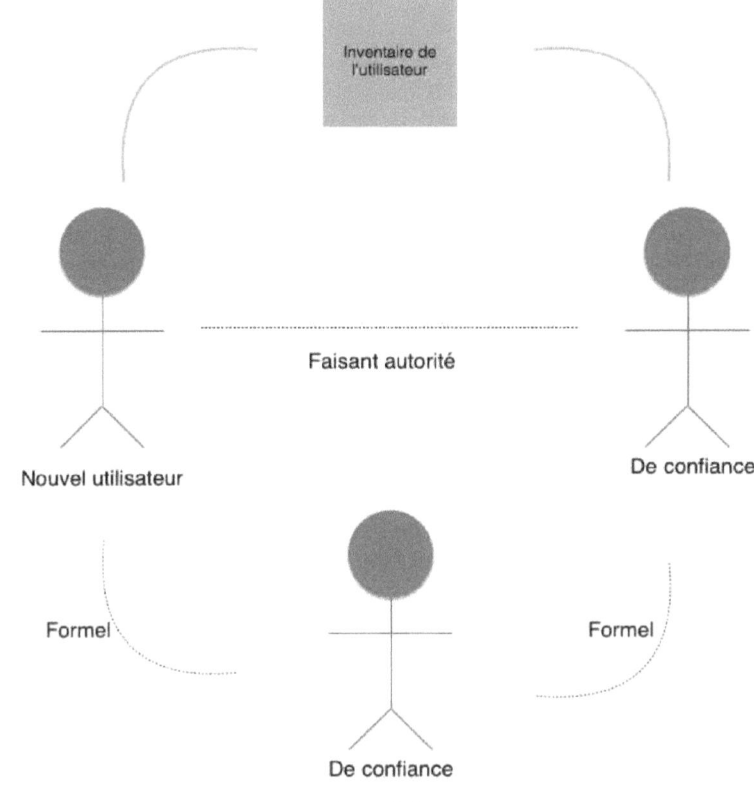

Figure 6-1

Expectations

There is usually a lot of information available before starting a digital identity. It is desirable to use as much information as possible. These expectations are similar to those set in a typical zero trust network; they are simply accumulated and imposed by humans.

These expectations can range from the language(s) spoken to the home address printed on their ID card, with many other creative examples in between. A thorough company may choose to use even the information learned from a background check to set real-world expectations. Humans use methods like this every day to authenticate each other (both casually and formally), and therefore, these methods are mature and reliable.

Store identity

Since we need to bridge the gap between the identity of the physical world and the virtual world, the identity must be transformed into bits. These bits are very sensitive and often need to be stored permanently. Therefore, we will discuss how to store this data to ensure its security.

User directories

To trust users, systems generally need centralized records of those users. The presence of someone in such a directory is the basis on which any future authentication will occur. Centralizing all this highly sensitive data is a challenge that unfortunately cannot be avoided.

A zero-trust network uses enriched user data to make better authentication decisions. Directories store traditional information such as usernames, phone numbers, and organizational roles, as well as extended information such as the intended location of the user or the public key of an X.509 certificate issued to them.

Due to **the sensitive nature of stored user data, it is best not to store all information in one database**. User information is generally not considered secret, but becomes sensitive when used to make authorization decisions. In addition, having extensive knowledge of all users of a system can pose a privacy risk. For example, a system that stores the last known location of all users could be used to spy on users. Stored user data can also pose a security risk if that data can be exploited to attack another system. Consider systems that ask users for factual information to validate their identity.

Instead of storing all user information in a single database, consider dividing the data into several isolated databases. Ideally, these databases should only be exposed via a constrained API, which limits the information disclosed. In the best case, the raw data is never disclosed, but assertions can be made about a user by the application that has access to the data. For example, a system that stores the previous known location of a user may expose the following APIs:
- Is the user currently or likely to be near these coordinates?
- How often does the user change location?

Directory maintenance

Keeping user directories accurate is essential to the security of a zero-trust network. Users are expected to come and go over the lifetime of a network system, so good integration procedures must be created to keep the system accurate.

Wherever possible, it is best to integrate technical identity systems (LDAP or local user accounts) with organizational systems. For example, a company may have human resources systems to track employees joining or leaving the company. These two data sources are expected to be consistent with each other, but unless there is a system that has integrated the two or verifies their contents, the data sets will quickly diverge. Creating automated processes to connect these systems is an effort that will quickly pay off.

The case of two divergent identity systems raises an important point - which system is authoritative? Clearly, one system must be the identity system of record, but this choice must be made based on the needs of the organization. It does not matter which system is chosen, only the authoritative one and all other identity systems draw their data from the system of record.

Minimizing stored data can be useful

A system of record for identity does not need to contain all identity information. Based on our previous discussion, it may be preferable to voluntarily segment the user data. The registration system should only store information that is essential to identify an individual. This could be as simple as storing a username and personal information so that the user can retrieve their identity if they forget it. Derived systems can use this authority ID to store additional user information.

When to authenticate identity

Although authentication is mandatory in a Zero Trust network, it can be applied intelligently to significantly enhance security while minimizing inconvenience to users.

While it might be tempting (and even logical) to adopt a position of "It's not supposed to be easy; it's supposed to be secure", user convenience is among the most important factors in designing a zero-trust network. Security technologies that have a poor user experience are often systematically weakened and undermined by their own users. A poor experience will discourage the user from engaging with the technology, and shortcuts to bypass the application will be taken more often.

Authentication for trust

The act of authenticating a user is, in essence, the system seeking to validate that the user is who they say they are. As you will learn in the next section, different authentication methods have different levels of strength, and some are stronger when combined with others. Because these authentication mechanisms are never absolute, we can assign a certain level of confidence to the result of the operation.

For example, you may only need a password to log into a subscription music service, but your investment account probably requires an additional password and code. That's because investing is a sensitive operation: the system must trust that the user is genuine. On the other hand, the music service is not as sensitive and chooses not to require an additional code, because that would be inconvenient.

By extension, a user can pass additional forms of authentication to raise their level of trust. This can be done specifically when needed. A user whose approval score has eroded below the requirements of a particular application may be asked for additional evidence which, if accepted, will increase trust to acceptable levels.

This is far from a foreign concept. It can be seen in common use today. Asking users to re-enter their passwords before performing a sensitive operation is an excellent example of this concept in action. It should be noted, however, that the amount of trust that can be gained through authentication mechanisms alone should not be untied. Otherwise, the consequences of poor device security and other unwanted signals can be eliminated.

Trust as an authentication driver

Since authentication derives trust, and our main goal is not to drag users frivolously through challenges, it makes sense to use the trust score as the mechanism that enforces authentication requirements. This means that a user should not be prompted to authenticate further if their trust score is high enough and, conversely, a user should be prompted to authenticate when their score is too low. This means that, rather than selecting particular actions that require additional authentication, a required score should be assigned and the trust score itself should be allowed to drive the authentication flow and requirements. This gives the system the ability to select a combination of methods to achieve the goal, potentially reducing invasiveness by putting into context the level of sensitivity and knowledge of the reliability of each method.

This approach is fundamentally different from traditional authentication design approaches, which seek to designate the most sensitive areas and actions and authenticate them in a more cumbersome manner, perhaps despite prior authentication and trust accumulation. In some respects, the traditional approach can be likened to perimeter security, in which sensitive actions must pass a particular test, after which no additional protection is present. Instead, using the trust score to drive these decisions removes arbitrary authentication requirements and installs adaptive authentication and authorization that is only encountered when necessary.

The use of multiple channels

When authenticating and authorizing a request, using multiple channels to reach the requester can be very effective. One-time codes provide an additional factor, especially when the code generating system is on a separate device. Push notifications provide similar functionality using an active connection to a mobile device. There are many applications of this idea, and they can take many forms.

Depending on the use case, it is possible to choose to leverage multiple channels as part of a digital authentication scheme. Alternatively, these channels can be used solely as an authorization component, where an applicant can be asked to approve a risky transaction. Both uses are effective, although the user experience is (as always) taken into account in deciding when and where to apply them.

Channel security

Communication channels are built with different degrees of authentication and trust. When operating multiple channels, it is important to understand what trust should be placed on the channel itself. This will determine which channels are selected and when. For example, spinning code devices are only as secure as the system used to distribute them or the identification verification required to physically obtain one from your administrator. Similarly, a prompt via a corporate chat system is only as strong as the credentials required to log in. Be sure to use a different channel than the one you are trying to authenticate/authorize in the first place.

Leveraging multiple channels is effective not because it is difficult to compromise one channel, but because it is difficult to compromise multiple channels. We'll talk more about these points in the next section.

Caching identity and trust

Session caching is a relatively mature technology that is well documented, so we won't spend too much time talking about it, but it is important to point out some design choices that are important for secure operation in a trustless network.

Frequent validation of client authorization is essential. It is one of the only mechanisms that allows the control plane to make changes in the data plane applications due to trust changes. The more often this can be done, the better. Some implementations allow all queries with the control plane. While this is ideal, it may not be a realistic prospect, depending on your situation.

Many applications validate SSO tokens only at the beginning of a session and then set their own tokens. This mode of operation removes session control from the control plane and is generally undesirable. Authorizing requests with control plane tokens rather than application tokens allows us to easily revoke when trust levels fluctuate or erode.

How to authenticate identity

Now that we know when to authenticate, let's consider how to authenticate a user. Common wisdom, which is also applicable in zero-trust networks, is that there are three ways to identify a user:

- *Something they know*
  Knowledge that only the user has (for example, a password).
- *Something they have*
  A physical identifier that the user can provide (for example, a token with a time token).
- *Something they are*
  A feature inherent to the user (for example, a fingerprint or a retina).

We can authenticate a user using one or more of these methods. The method or methods chosen will depend on the level of trust required. For high-risk operations, which require multiple authentication factors, it is best to choose methods that are not in the same group of something you know, something you have, or something you are. This is because attack vectors are usually similar within a particular group.

For example, a hardware token (something you have) can be stolen and then used by anyone. If we combine this token with a second token, it is very likely that the two devices will be close to each other and stolen together.

The factors to be used together vary depending on the device the user is using. For example, on a desktop computer, a password (something you know) and a hardware token (something you have) is a strong combination that should generally be preferred. For a mobile device, however, a fingerprint (something you are) and a secret phrase (something you know) might be preferred.

Physical security is a requirement for trusted users

This section focuses on technological means of authenticating a user's identity, but it is important to recognize that users may be compelled to thwart these mechanisms. A user may be threatened with physical harm to force them to disclose their credentials or grant access to someone under a trusted account. Behavioral analysis and historical trends can help mitigate these attempts, although they remain an effective attack vector.

Something you know: passwords

Passwords are the most common form of authentication used in computer systems today. Although often maligned because of the tendency of users to choose bad passwords, this authentication mechanism offers a very valuable advantage: when done properly, it is an effective method of asserting that a user's mind is present.

A good password has the following characteristics:

- *It's a long time*
  A recent NIST password standard stipulates a minimum of 8 characters, but passwords longer than 20 characters are common among security-conscious individuals. Secret phrases are often encouraged to help users remember a longer password.
- *It is difficult to guess*

Users tend to overestimate their ability to choose truly random passwords, so generating passwords from random number generators can be a good way to choose a strong password.

- *It is not reused*

Passwords must be validated against certain data stored in a service. When passwords are reused, the confidentiality of that password is as strong as the weakest storage used.

Choosing long, hard-to-guess passwords for every service or application a user interacts with is a high bar that users must meet. As a result, users are well served to use a password manager to store their passwords. Using this tool will allow users to choose passwords that are much harder to guess and thus limit the damage caused by a data breach.

When creating a service that authenticates passwords, it is important to follow best practices. Passwords should never be stored or recorded directly. Instead, a cryptographic hash of the password should be stored. The cost of brute force password cracking (usually expressed in time and/or memory) is determined by the strength of the hash algorithm. NIST periodically publishes standards documents that include recommended password procedures. As computers become more powerful, the current recommendations change. Therefore, it is best to consult industry best practices when selecting algorithms.

Something you have: TOTP

Time-based one-time passwords, or TOTPs, are an authentication standard where a constantly changing code is provided by the user. RFC 6238 defines the standard implemented in hardware devices and software applications. Mobile applications are often used to generate the code, which works well because users tend to have their phones nearby.

Whether you are using an application or a hardware device, TOTP requires the sharing of a random secret value between the user and the service. This secret and the current time are passed through a cryptographic hash and then truncated to produce the code to enter. As long as the device and server roughly agree on the current time, a corresponding code confirms that the user is in possession of the shared key.

The storage of the shared key is essential, both on the device and on the authentication server. Losing control of this secret will permanently break this authentication mechanism. The RFC recommends encrypting the key using a hardware device such as a TPM, and then limiting access to the encrypted data.

Exposing the shared key to a mobile device puts it in greater danger than on a server. The device can connect to a malicious endpoint that could extract the key. To mitigate this vector, an alternative to TOTP is to send a random code to the user's mobile phone over an encrypted channel. This code is then entered on another device to authenticate that the user is in possession of their mobile phone.

SMS is not a secure communication channel

Sending a random code to the user for authentication requires that the authentication code be reliably delivered to the intended device and not exposed in transit. Systems have previously sent random codes in the form of an SMS message, but the SMS system does not provide sufficient guarantees to protect the random code in transit. The use of SMS for this system is therefore not recommended.

Something you have: Certificates

Another method of authenticating users is to generate X.509 certificates per user. The certificate is derived from a strong private key and then signed using the private key of the organization that provided the certificate. The certificate cannot be modified without invalidating the organization's signature, so the certificate can be used as a right of access to any service configured to approve the organization's signature.

An X.509 certificate is intended for consumption by a computer, not humans, so it can provide much richer detail when presented to an authentication service. For example, a system can encode metadata about the user in the certificate and then approve that data since it was signed by a trusted organization. This can reduce the need to create a directory of trusted users in less mature networks.

The use of certificates to identify users relies heavily on the secure storage of these certificates. It is highly preferable to both generate and store the private key component on dedicated hardware in order to prevent digital theft. We will discuss this further in the next section.

Something you have: security tokens

Security tokens are hardware devices used primarily for user authentication, but they have additional applications. These devices are not mass storage devices storing credentials that have been provisioned elsewhere. Instead, the hardware itself generates a private key. This credential never leaves the token. The user's device interacts with the hardware's APIs to perform cryptographic operations on behalf of the user, proving that it is in possession of the hardware.

As the security industry progresses, organizations are increasingly turning to hardware mechanisms to authenticate user identity. Devices such as smart cards or Yubikeys can provide affirmation for a particular identity. By tying identity to hardware, the risk that a particular user's credentials can be duplicated and stolen without their knowledge is greatly mitigated, as physical theft would be required.

Storing a private key in hardware is by far the most secure storage method we have today. The stored private key can then be used as a medium for many different types of authentication schemes. Traditionally, they have been used in conjunction with X.509, but a new protocol called Universal 2nd Factor (U2F) is being adopted rapidly. U2F provides an alternative to fullblown PKI, offering a lightweight challenge-response protocol designed for use by Web services. Whichever authentication scheme you choose, if it relies on asymmetric cryptography, you should probably use a security token.

While these hardware tokens can provide strong protections against the theft of credentials, they cannot guarantee that the token itself is not stolen or misused. Therefore, it is important to recognize that while these tokens are excellent tools for building a secure system, they cannot completely replace a user asserting their identity. If we want the strongest guarantee that a particular user is who they say they are, the use of a security key with additional authentication factors (e.g., a password or biometric sensor) is always highly recommended.

Something you are : Biometrics

Asserting identity by recognizing the physical characteristics of the user is called biometrics. Biometrics is becoming more common as advanced sensors make their way into the devices we use every day. This authentication system offers greater convenience and potentially a more secure system, if biometric signals, such as the following, are used

appropriately.
- Footprints -
   Handprints -
   Retinal scan -
   Speech analysis -
   Recognition of
face

The use of biometrics may seem like the ideal authentication method. After all, authenticating a user validates that they are who they say they are. What could be better than measuring a user's physical characteristics? While biometrics is a useful addition to system security, there are some drawbacks that should not be overlooked.

Authentication via biometrics relies on the precise measurement of a physical characteristic. If an attacker is able to fool the scanner, they can get in. Fingerprints, being a common biometric, are left on everything a person touches. Attacks against fingerprint readers have been demonstrated - attackers obtain images of a latent fingerprint, then 3D print a fake, which the scanner accepts.

In addition, biometric identification information cannot be rotated, as it is a physical feature. They may also present an accessibility problem if, for example, an individual was born without fingerprints (a condition known as adermatoglyphia) or if they lost their fingers in an accident.

Finally, biometrics can present surprising legal challenges compared to other authentication mechanisms. **In the United States, for example, a citizen can be compelled by a court to provide his or her fingerprints to authenticate on a device, but cannot be compelled to divulge his or her password, under its Fifth Amendment against self-incrimination.**

Out-of-band authentication

Out-of-band authentication deliberately uses a communication channel separate from the original channel used by the user to authenticate that request. For example, a user logging into a website for the first time on a device may receive a phone call to validate the request. By using out-of-band verification, a service is able to increase the difficulty of breaking into an account, since the attacker would also need to control the out-of-band communication channel.

Out-of-band controls can take many forms. These forms should be chosen according to the desired level of strength for each interaction: - A passive email can inform users of potentially sensitive actions that have recently taken place.
- Confirmation may be required before an application is completed. Confirmation may be a simple "yes", or it may involve entering a TOTP code.
- A third party may be contacted to confirm the requested action.

When used properly, out-of-band authentication can be a useful tool for enhancing system security. As with all authentication mechanisms, a certain level of taste is required in choosing the right authentication mechanism and frequency, depending on the application at hand.

Single Sign On

Given the large number of services that users interact with, the industry would prefer to decouple authentication from the end services. Having decoupled authentication brings benefits to both the service and the user:

- Users only need to authenticate with one service.
- The authentication material is stored in a dedicated service, which may have stricter security standards.
- Security credentials in fewer locations mean less risk and easier rotations.

Single sign-on (SSO) is a fairly mature concept. Under SSO, users authenticate themselves with a centralized authority, after which they will typically receive a token. This token is then used in further communication with secure services. When the service receives a request, it contacts the authentication authority over a secure channel to validate the token provided by the client.

This is in contrast to decentralized authentication. A zero-trust network using decentralized authentication will use the control plane to push credentials and access policy into the data plane. This allows the data plane to perform authentication itself, when and where needed, while continuing to be supported by the policy and control plane concern. This approach is sometimes preferred over a more mature SSO approach because it does not require the execution of an additional service, although it introduces enough complexity that it is not recommended.

SSO tokens should be validated as often as possible by the centralized authority. Each call to the control plane to authorize a single sign-on token provides the opportunity to revoke access or change the approval level (known to the caller).

A popular mode of operation involves the service making its own connection, with SSO authentication. The main drawback of this approach is that it allows the control plane to authorize the request only once and lets the application make all other decisions. Trust variance and invalidation is a key aspect of a zero trust network, so decisions to follow this model should not be taken lightly.

Existing options

SSO has been around for a long time and as such there are many mature protocols/technologies to support it, including the most popular:
SAML
- Kerberos
CASE

It is essential that authentication remain a control plane issue in a zero-trust network. As such, when designing authentication systems in a zero-trust network, aim for control plane accountability as much as possible, and validate authorization with the control plane as often as reasonably possible.

Move to a local authentication solution

```
~ $ echo 'this is a secret' | ssss-split -n 5 -t 2
Generating shares using a (2,5) scheme with dynamic security level.
Enter the secret, at most 128 ASCII characters: Using a 128 bit security level.
1-4054162f42f328c2ecbff990e9e1996f
2-93285deac4d6406cde841b05b350f61f
3-22039b5646ca98093092ba897ac02cb0
4-35d0ca61c89c9130baf3de2f06322866
5-84fb0cdd4a80495554e57fa3cfa2f2c9
~ $ ssss-combine -t 2
Enter 2 shares separated by newlines:
Share [1/2]: 5-84fb0cdd4a80495554e57fa3cfa2f2c9
Share [2/2]: 4-35d0ca61c89c9130baf3de2f06322866
Resulting secret: this is a secret
```

Figure 6-2

Local authentication extended to remote services is another authentication mechanism that is increasingly becoming a possibility. In this system, users authenticate their presence to a trusted device, and then the device can attest to that identity with a remote service. Open standards such as the FIDO Alliance's UAF standard use asymmetric cryptography and local device authentication schemes (e.g., passwords and biometrics) to shift trust away from a large number of services to relatively few user-controlled endpoints.

UAF, in some ways, is very similar to a password manager. However, instead of storing passwords, it stores private keys. The authentication service then receives the user's public key and can confirm that the user has the private key.

By moving authentication to a local smart device, a number of advantages arise: - Replay attacks can be mitigated via a challenge-and-response system.
- Man-in-the-middle attacks can be thwarted by the fact that the authentication service refuses to sign the challenge unless it comes from the same domain as the one visited by the user.
- Reuse of credentials is non-existent, as the credentials per service can be generated trivially.

Authentication and authorization of a group

Almost all systems have a small set of actions or applications that must be closely monitored. The amount of risk one is willing to tolerate in this area will vary from application to application, although there is virtually no lower limit.

One of the risks you pass when approaching zero is the amount of trust in a single human being. Just like in real life, it's often desirable to get consent from multiple people to authorize a particularly sensitive action. There are many ways to accomplish this in the digital realm, and the coolest part is that we can guarantee it cryptographically!

Shamir's Secret Share

Shamir secret sharing is a system for distributing a single secret among a group of individuals. The algorithm breaks the original secret into n parts, which can then be distributed (Figure 6-2). Depending on how the algorithm was set up when the coins were generated, it takes k parts to recompute the original secret value.

When protecting large amounts of data using Shamir secret sharing, a symmetric encryption key is usually split and distributed instead of using the algorithm directly on the data.

This is because the size of the secret to be split must be smaller than some of the data used in the secret sharing algorithm.

A Unix / Linux version of this algorithm is called "ssss". Similar applications and libraries exist for other operating systems or programming languages.

Red October

Cloudflare's Red October project is another approach to implementing group authentication to access shared data. This web service uses layered asymmetric cryptography to encrypt data so that a number of users must come together to decrypt the data. The encrypted data is not actually stored on the server. Instead, only the user's public/private key pairs (encrypted with a password chosen by the user) are stored.

When data is submitted for encryption, a random encryption key is generated to encrypt the data. This encryption key is then itself encrypted using unique combinations of user-specific encryption keys based on a user-requested unlocking policy.

In the simplest case, one user may encrypt some data so that two people in a larger group must work together to decrypt the data. In this scenario, the encryption key of the original encrypted data is therefore doubly encrypted with each unique pair of user encryption keys.

About DNS root zone signing

An interesting example of a group authentication procedure is the DNS root zone signing ceremony. This ceremony is used to generate the root keys on which all DNSSEC approval is based. If the root key is compromised, the reliability of the entire DNSSEC system will be compromised, so the root key ceremony is specifically designed to mitigate this risk.

The first ceremony took place on June 16, 2010 and a new ceremony is held every quarter. The ceremony uses seven actors, each with a different role. The ceremony mitigates the risk of compromise to one chance in a million, assuming a 5% dishonesty rate among the actors in the ceremony. A strict procedural document is generated to organize the ceremony. HSMs, biometric scanners and gap systems are used to protect the digital key. At the end, a new public/private key pair is generated and signed, extending the trust anchor of the Internet for another quarter.

You can learn more about the signing ceremony on the Cloudflare website, or you can see the documents for each ceremony on the IANA website.

See something, Say something

Users of a Zero Trust network, such as devices, must actively participate in system security. Organizations have traditionally formed dedicated teams to focus on system security. These teams, more often than not, took this mandate to mean that they alone were responsible for the security of the system. Changes had to be verified by them to ensure that the security of the system was not compromised. This approach produces an adversarial relationship between the security team and the rest of the organization and, as a result, reduces security.

A better approach is to build a culture of collaboration towards system safety. Users should be encouraged to speak up if something they are doing or seeing is odd or dangerous, no matter how small. This knowledge sharing will give better context to the threats the security team is working to defend against. Reporting phishing emails, even when users don't interact with them, can inform the security team if a determined attacker is trying to infiltrate the network.

Lost or stolen devices should be reported immediately. Security teams may want to consider providing users with a means of alerting them day or night if their device is lost.

When responding to user tips or alerts, security teams need to be aware of how their response to the incident affects the organization more broadly. A user who is ashamed of having lost a device will be less likely to report the loss in a timely manner in the future. Similarly, a false alarm late at night should be respected. If possible, try to bias the organization towards over-reporting.

Confidence signals

Historical user activity is a rich source of data for determining the reliability of a user's current actions. A system can be built that mines the user's activity to build a model of expected behavior. This system then compares current behavior with this model as a method of computing a user's trust score.

Humans tend to have predictable access patterns. Most people will not try to authenticate multiple times per second. They are also unlikely to try to authenticate hundreds of times. These types of accesses are extremely suspicious and are often mitigated by active methods such as CAPTCHAs (automated challenges that only a human can answer) or locked accounts. To reduce false positives, actively ban fairly high bars. Including this activity in an overall threat assessment score can help catch suspicious, but not obviously bad, behavior. Examination of access patterns need not be limited to authentication attempts. User application usage patterns can also reveal malicious intent. Most users typically have fairly limited roles in an organization and therefore only need access to a subset of data that is accessible to them. In an effort to increase security, organizations will begin to remove access rights from employees unless they absolutely need the access to do their job. However, this type of restrictive access control can impact the organization's ability to respond quickly to single events. System administrators are a class of users who have broad access, thus weakening this approach as a defense mechanism. Instead of choosing between these two extremes, we can assess the user's activity globally, and then use their score to determine if they are still trusted to access a particularly sensitive resource. It is always important to have downtime in the system - these are the less obvious cases where the system needs to trust users, but verify their trustworthiness through logged activity.

Lists of known bad traffic sources, such as the one provided by Spamhaus, can be another useful signal for a user's trustworthiness. Traffic that originates from these addresses and attempts to use a particular user's identity may point to a potentially compromised user.

Geolocation can be another useful signal for determining a user's trustworthiness. We can compare the user's current location with previously visited locations to determine if they are out of the ordinary. Did the user's device suddenly appear in a new location within a time frame that they could not reasonably travel? If the user has multiple devices, are they reporting conflicting addresses? Geolocation can be false or misleading, so systems should not weigh too heavily. Sometimes users forget devices at home or the geolocation databases are simply incorrect.

Summary

This chapter has focused on how to establish trust in users of a system. We talked about the definition of identity and the importance of having a reference authority when verifying a user's identity in the system. Users must be entered into a system to have an identity, so we talked about some ideal ways to bootstrap their identity.

Identity has to be stored somewhere, and that system is a very valuable target for attackers. We talked about how to store data securely, the importance of limiting the scope of data stored in one place, and keeping the stored identity up to date as users come and go.

With the authority identity defined and stored, we turned our attention to authenticating users who claim to have a particular identity. Authentication can be an inconvenience to users, so we discussed the timing of user authentication.

We don't want users to be inundated with authentication requests, as this will increase the likelihood of them accidentally authenticating against a malicious service. Therefore, finding the right balance is critical.

There are many ways to authenticate users, so we dug into the basic concepts. We discussed several authentication mechanisms that are in use today. We also looked at some authentication mechanisms that are emerging as system security practices respond to threats.

Often, increasing trust in a user system involves creating procedures where multiple users play a role to achieve a goal. We discussed group authentication and authorization systems such as "two-person rules", which can be used to secure highly sensitive data. We also discussed building a culture of awareness in an organization by encouraging users to report suspicious activity.

Finally, zero-trust networks can exploit user activity logs to create a profile of users to compare when evaluating new actions. We have listed some useful signals that can be used to build this profile.

The next chapter examines how trust in applications can be built.

Chapter 7: trusted applications

Marc Andreessen, a notable Silicon Valley investor, has stated that "software is eating the world." In many ways, that statement has never been more true. It's the software running in your datacenter that does all the magic, and as such, it's no secret that we want to trust its execution.

Code, executed on a trusted device, will be faithfully executed. A trusted device is a prerequisite for code approval, which we discussed in Chapter 5. However, even with our secure execution environment, we still have work to do to ensure that code executed on a device is trusted.

As such, trusting the device is just half the story. You also have to trust the code and the programmers who wrote it. In the interest of ensuring the integrity of a race.

Establishing trust in code requires that: - The people producing the code are themselves trusted - The code has been faithfully processed to produce a trustworthy application - Trusted applications are faithfully deployed on the infrastructure to be run - Trusted applications are continuously monitored in an attempt to constrain

the application with malicious actions

This chapter will discuss approaches to securing each of these steps, with an emphasis on the legacy of trust from human to production application.

Understanding the application pipeline

The creation, delivery and execution of code in a computer system is a very sensitive chain of events. These systems are an attractive target for adversaries because of their ability to gain greater access. Attack vectors exist at each stage, and subversion at these stages can be very difficult to detect. Therefore, we must ensure that each link in this chain (shown in Figure 7-1) is secured in a way that makes subversion detectable.

This process is similar to supply chain security, the collective efforts of governments around the world to enhance security. Ensuring that military equipment is solidly built/sourced is critical to ensuring the effectiveness of the fighting force, and the creation and delivery of software is no different.

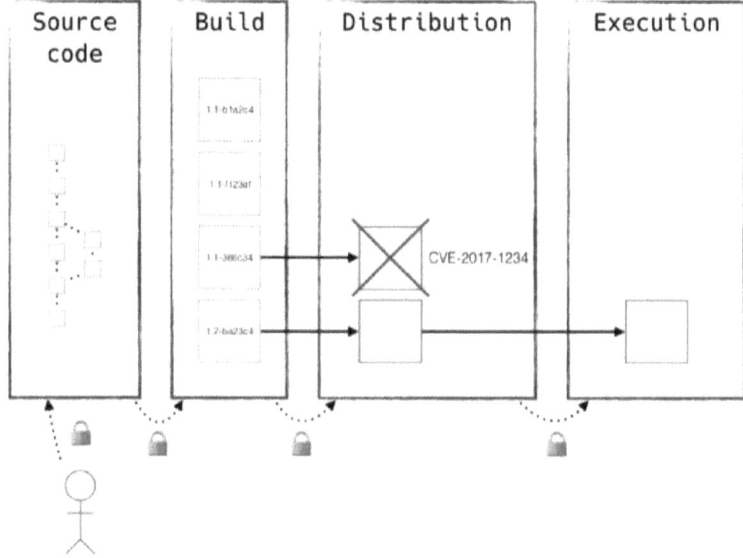

Figure 7-1

Criticality of the supply chain

In 2007, the Israeli government conducted an air strike against a suspected nuclear facility in Syria. One of the many mysteries surrounding this strike was the sudden failure of Syrian radar systems, providing the Israelis with cover. The failure of these radar systems, which were supposed to be state-of-the-art, is now widely attributed to a hardware kill switch hidden in a commercial chip used by the radar equipment. Although never verified, stories like this underscore the importance of secure supply chains, whether for hardware or software.

In support of a secure software delivery chain, each step in the process should be fully verifiable with cryptographic validation occurring at each critical point. In general, these steps can be broken down into four distinct phases:
- source code
- build/compilation
- distribution
- execution

Let's start by trusting the source code itself.

Source of confidence

Source code is the first step in the execution of any software. To put it very simply, it is difficult to trust source code that is written by an untrusted human. Even with a rigorous code audit, it is still possible for a malicious developer to encode (and hide!) a vulnerability in plain sight. In fact, there is even a well-known competition dedicated to this dark art. While well-meaning developers may inadvertently add weakness to an application, a zero-trust network will focus on identifying malicious use rather than removing trust from those users.

Putting aside the trusted developer problem for a minute, we still face the problem of securely storing and distributing the source code itself. Typically, source code is stored in a centralized code repository, against which many developers interact and commit work. These repositories must also be strictly controlled, especially if they are used directly by systems that build/compile the code in question.

Securing the repository

Maintaining traditional security approaches when securing a software repository is still effective and does not preclude adding more advanced security features. This includes basic principles such as the principle of least access, where users only have as much access to the repository as necessary to accomplish the current task. In practice, this usually translates into highly limited/restricted write access.

While this approach is still valid and recommended, the story has changed a bit with the introduction of distributed source control. With the code repository living in multiple locations, it is not always possible to secure a single centralized entity. In this case, however, there remains an analogue for that centralized repository - the system storing the code from which the build system reads.

In this case, it is still highly desirable to protect this system by traditional means; however, the problem becomes more difficult because code can enter the distributed repository in many ways. The logical extension, therefore, is that securing the build source repository alone is not enough.

Authentic code and audit trail

Many version control systems (VCSs), particularly those that are distributed, store source history using cryptographic techniques. This approach, called content addressable storage, uses cryptographic hashing of stored content as an identifier for that object in a database, rather than its location or coordinates. It is possible to see how a source file can be hashed and stored in such a database, thus ensuring that any change in the source file results in a new hash.

This property means that the files are stored immutably: it is impossible to modify the content of the files once stored.

Some VCS systems take this storage mechanism a step further by storing the history itself as an object in the content addressable database. Git, a popular distributed VCS project, stores the commit history in the repository as a directed acyclic graph (DAG). Commits are objects in the database, storing details such as commit time, author, and ancestor commit IDs. By storing the cryptographic hashes of ancestor commits on each commit itself, we form a Merkle tree, which allows us to cryptographically validate that the commit chain is not modified (Figure 7-2).

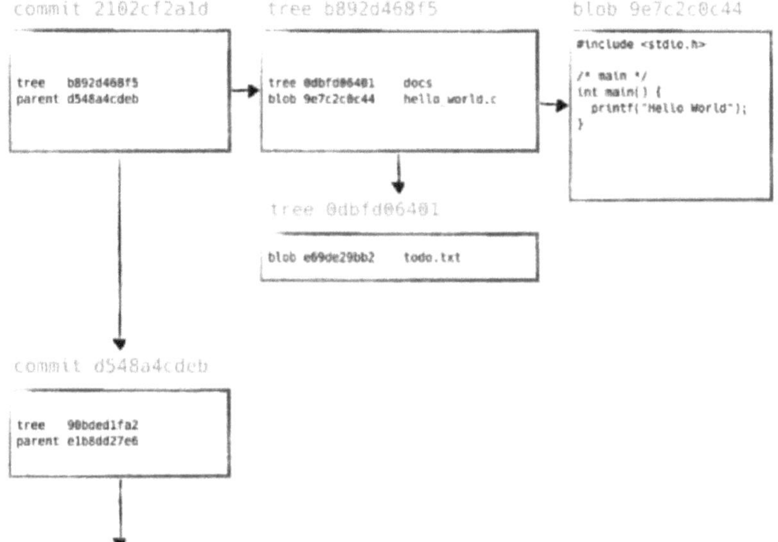

Figure 7-2

If a validation in the DAG were to be changed, its update will affect all descending validations in the graph, changing the content of each validation, and by extension, its identifier. With the source history distributed to many contributors, the system gains another beneficial property: it is impossible to change the history without other contributors noticing.

Storing the DAG in this way gives us a tamper-proof history: it is impossible to change the history in a subversive way. However, this storage does nothing to ensure that new commits in the history are authorized and authentic.

Imagine for a moment that a trusted developer is persuaded to remove a malicious commit in their local repository before pushing it to the official repository. That commit is now in the repository based on the trusted developer's push access. More worryingly, the author metadata is simply text: a malicious author can put any details he wants in this field (a fact that was amusingly used to make commits appear by Linus Torvalds on GitHub).

To guard against this attack vector, Git has the ability to sign commits and tags using a trusted developer's GPG key. Tags, which point to the head commit in a particular history, can be signed using a GPG key to ensure the authenticity of a release. Signed commits go a step further and authenticate the entire Git history, making it impossible for an attacker to impersonate another committer without first stealing that committer's GPG key.

Signed source code clearly offers significant advantages and should be used whenever possible. It provides robust code authentication not only to humans, but also to machines. This is particularly important if CI/CD systems build and deploy code automatically. A fully signed history allows build systems to cryptographically authenticate the code as reliable before compiling it for deployment.

At first, there was nothing

Many repositories start with unsigned releases and then move to signed releases later. In this case, the first commitment to be signed is essentially the approval of all the commitments that preceded it. This is important to understand, as you may want to audit at this time. That said, the overhead or difficulty of performing such an audit should not deter or delay the transition to signed code; the audit, if you choose to do so, can be performed in a timely manner.

Code Notice

As we learned in Chapter 6, it can be dangerous to concentrate powerful capabilities on a single user. This is no different when considering source code contributions. Signed contributions allow us to authenticate the developer validating the code, but do not guarantee that the validated code is correct or secure. Of course, we place non-trivial trust in the developer, although this does not mean that the developer should unilaterally validate code for sensitive projects.

To mitigate this risk, most mature organizations implement a code review process. Under code review, all contributions must be approved by one or more additional developers. This

This simple process not only greatly improves the quality of the software, but also reduces the speed at which vulnerabilities are introduced, whether intentionally or accidentally.

Building with confidence

Build servers are frequently the target of persistent threats and for good reason. They have high access and produce code that is executed directly in production. Detecting artifacts (a script, an image, etc) that have been compromised during the build phase can be very difficult, so it is important to apply strong protections to these services.

The risk

In trusting a building system, there are generally three things we want to affirm:
- The source code he built is the code we intend to build.
- The build/configuration process is as we planned.
- The construction itself was carried out faithfully, without manipulation.

Build systems can ingest signed code and produce output signed, but the function(s) applied between them (i.e., the construct itself) is usually not cryptographically protected - this is the most significant attack vector.

This particular vector is powerful, as shown in Figure 7-3. Without the right processes and validation, subversion of this type can be difficult or impossible to detect. For example, imagine a compromised CI/CD system that ingests signed C code and compiles it into a signed binary, which is then distributed and executed in production. Production systems can validate that the binary is signed, but would have no way of knowing if additional malicious code was compiled during the build process. In this way, a seemingly secure system can successfully execute malicious code in production without detection. Perhaps even worse, consumers are fooled into thinking that the output is safe.

Because of the sensitive nature of the construction process, outsourcing responsibility must be carefully evaluated. Things like repeatable builds can help identify compromises in this area (more on that later), but can't always prevent their distribution. Is this really something you want a third-party vendor to do for you? How much do you trust them? Their security position should be weighed against your own chance to be a high-value target.

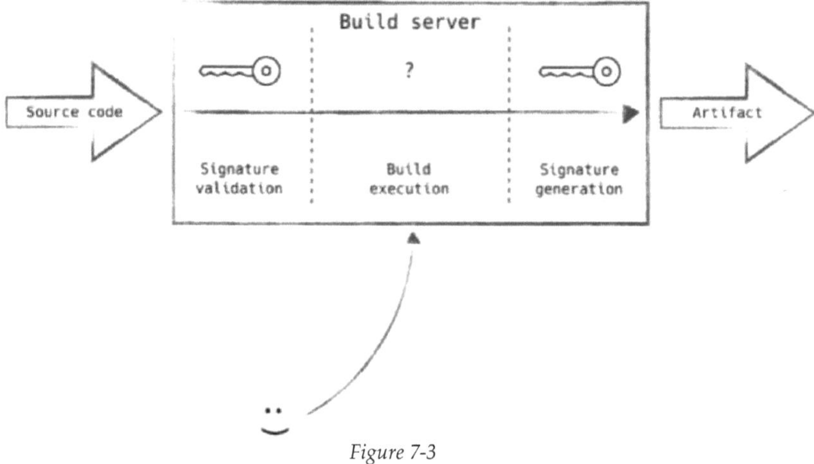

Figure 7-3

<u>**Host security is always important**</u>

This section focuses on securing the various stages of the software build process, but it is important to note that the security of the build servers themselves is still important. We can secure the input, output, and configuration of the build, but if the build server is compromised, it can no longer be trusted to faithfully perform its tasks. Reproducible builds, immutable hosts, and the zero-trust model itself can help in this regard.

Secure entry, secure exit

If we think of the construction system as a trusting operation, it is clear that we must trust the input to that operation to produce a trusting output.

Let's start by trusting the input to the building system. We discussed mechanisms for trusting source control systems earlier. The build system, as a consumer of the version control system, is responsible for validating the trustworthiness of the source. The version control system must be accessible over an authenticated channel, typically TLS. Furthermore, for additional security guarantees, tags and/or validations must be signed and the build system must validate these signatures - or chain of signatures - before starting a build.

The build configuration is another important input to the build system. Attacking the build configuration could allow an attacker to direct the build system to a link to a malicious library. Even seemingly safe optimization indicators can be malicious in safety-critical code, where timing attack mitigation code can be accidentally optimized. Putting this configuration under source control, where it can be versioned and certified via signed validations, ensures that the build configuration is also a trusted input.

With the input sufficiently secure, we can turn our attention to the output of the construction process. The build system must sign the generated artifacts so that downstream systems can validate their authenticity. Build systems also typically generate cryptographic hashes of the build artifacts to guard against corruption or malicious attempts to replace the binaries once produced. Securing the build artifacts and hashes, and then distributing them to downstream users, completes the secure output of the generating system.

Reproducible constructions

Reproducible builds are the best tool we have to protect against subversion of the build pipeline. In short, software supporting reproducible builds is compiled deterministically, ensuring that the resulting binary is exactly the same for a given source code, no matter who built it. This is a very powerful property, as it allows multiple parties to examine the source code and produce identical builds, thereby gaining confidence that the build process used to generate a particular binary has not been tampered with.

This can be done in many ways, but it usually involves a codified build process, and allows developers to set up their own build environment to produce binaries that match the bit-for-bit distributed versions. With reproducible builds, one can "watch" the output of a CI/CD system, and compare its output to the locally compiled results. In this way, malicious interference or code injection during the build process can be easily detected. When combined with signed source code, we arrive at a fairly robust process that is able to authenticate both the source code and the binary produced by it.

Virtualized Build Environments Enabling Reproducible Builds

Having reproducible builds looks easy on paper, but reproducing a build binary so that it is byte for byte identical is a very difficult problem. Distributions have historically built packages inside a virtual file system (a chroot jail) to ensure that all build dependencies are captured in the build configuration. Virtual machines or containers can be useful tools to ensure that the build environment is completely isolated from the host running the build.

Decoupling of Release and Artifact

Immutable builds are essential to the security of a build and release system. Without them, replacement of a known good version is possible, opening the door to attacks targeting the underlying build artifact. This would allow an attacker to mask a "bad" version as a "good" version. For this reason, artifacts generated by build systems should have Write Once Read Many semantics.

Given the requirement for immutable artifacts, a natural tension arises with versioning these artifacts. Many projects prefer to use meaningful version numbers (e.g., semantic versions) in their releases to communicate the potential impact to downstream consumers with an upgrade of their software. This desire to attach meaning to the version number can be difficult to incorporate into a build system that must ensure that each version is immutable.

For example, when working on a major release, a project may have a misconfigured build that causes the build system to produce incorrectly. Maintainers are now faced with a choice. They can republish the release using a patch-level bump, or they can decide to change the rules and republish the same release using a new build artifact. Many projects choose the latter option, preferring the benefit of a clearer marketing story over the more correct reversion. This is a bad habit to get into when you consider the charade just described.

It is clear from this example that in both cases, two distinct build artifacts have been produced and the version number associated with the build artifact is a distinct choice for the project. Therefore, when creating a build system, it is preferable that the build system produce immutable versions independently of the publicly released version. A subsequent system (the distribution system) can handle version mapping to build versions of artifacts. This approach allows us to maintain immutable build artifacts without sacrificing usability or introducing poor security practices.

Confidence in distribution

The process of choosing which construction artifacts to deliver to downstream consumers is called distribution. The construction system produces many artifacts, some of which are destined for downstream consumption. Therefore, we need to ensure that the distribution system maintains control over which artifacts are ultimately delivered.

Promote an artifact

Based on our previous discussion of immutable building artifacts, promotion is the act of designating a building artifact as the authoritative version without changing the content of that artifact. This act itself should be immutable: once a version is assigned and released, it cannot be changed. Instead, a new artifact must be produced and released under an incrementally higher version number.

This constraint presents a chicken and egg scenario. Software typically includes a way to report its version number to the user, but if the version number is not assigned until later in the build process, how can this version information be added without modifying the build artifact?

A naive approach is to subtly modify the artifact during the promotion process, for example, by storing the version number in a trivially modified location in the build artifact. This approach, however, is not preferred. Instead, release engineers must establish a clear separation between the publicly released version number and the version number, which is an additional component of the release information. With this model, many build artifacts are produced that use the same release version, but each build is additionally marked with a unique build number (Figure 7-4). Releasing this version is therefore choosing which build artifact will be signed and distributed. Once such a release is made, all new releases must be configured to use the following target version number.

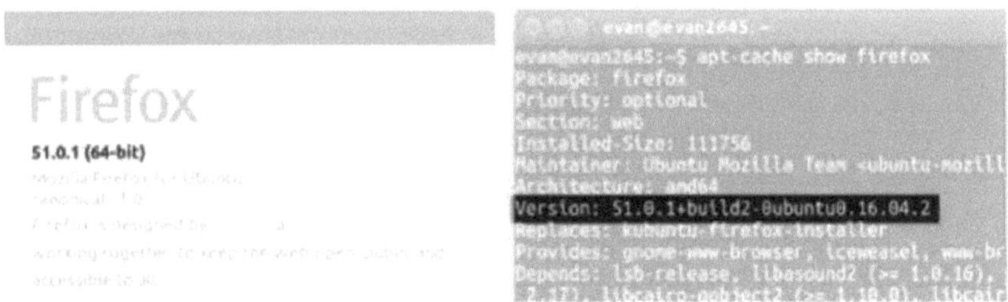

Figure 7-4

Of course, this promotion must be communicated to the consumer in a way that allows them to validate that they are in possession of the promoted build, not an intermediate and potentially flawed construct. There are several ways to do this, and it's largely a solved problem. One way is to sign promoted artifacts with a version key only, thus communicating to consumers that they have a promoted build. Another way to do this is to publish a signed manifest, describing the released versions and their cryptographic hashes. Many popular package distribution systems, such as APT, use this method to validate builds obtained from their distribution systems.

Distribution security

Software distribution is similar to electricity distribution, where electricity is generated by a centralized source and transported over a distribution system for delivery to a large consumer base. Unlike electricity, however, the integrity of the software produced must be protected as it travels through the distribution system, and allow the consumer to independently validate its integrity. There are a number of widely adopted distribution and package management systems, virtually all of which have protections in place around the distribution process and allow consumers to validate the authenticity of packages received through them. Throughout this section we will use the popular APT (Advanced Packaging Tool) package management software to illustrate how some of the concepts are implemented in real life, but it is important to keep in mind that there are many options available.

Integrity and authenticity

There are two main mechanisms used to assert integrity and authenticity in software distribution systems: hashing and signing. Hashing a software version involves computing and distributing a cryptographic hash representing the released binary, which the consumer can validate to ensure that the binary has not been changed since it left the developer's hands. Signing a release involves the author encrypting the hash of the release with their private key, which allows consumers to validate that the software was released by an authorized party. Both methods are effective and not necessarily mutually exclusive. To better understand how these methods can be applied in a distribution system, it is useful to examine the structure and security of an APT repository.

An APT repository contains three types of files: a Release file, a Packages file and the packages themselves. The packages file acts as an index to all the packages in the repository. It stores some metadata about each package contained in the repository, such as file names, descriptions and checksums. The checksum from this index is used to validate the integrity of the downloaded package before it is installed. This ensures integrity, assuring us that the contents have not changed in flight. It is, however, mostly only effective against corruption, as an attacker can simply modify the index hashes if the goal is to deliver modified software. This is where the release file comes in.

The Release file contains metadata about the repo itself (as opposed to the Packages file, which stores metadata about the packages it contains). This includes things like the name and version of the operating system distribution for which the repo is intended. It also includes a checksum of the Packages file, allowing the consumer to validate the integrity of the index, which in turn can validate the integrity of the packages we download. This is great, except that an attacker can simply modify the Release file with the updated hash of the Packages file and be on their way.

We therefore introduce cryptographic signatures (Figure 7-5).

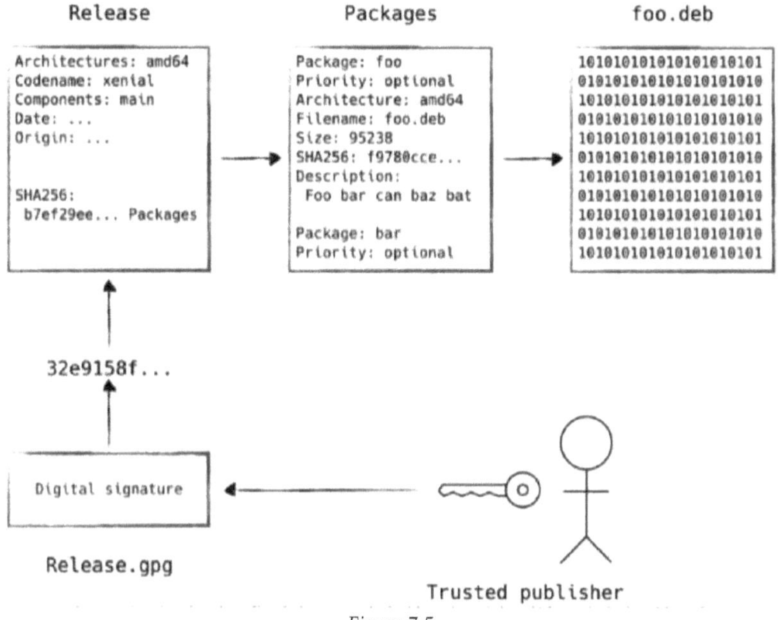

Figure 7-5

A signature provides not only integrity for the contents of the signed file (since a signature is included in the signature), but also authenticity, since successful decryption of the signature proves that the generating party was in the presence of the private key.

Using this principle, the software repo maintainer signs the Release file with a private key, to which there is a well known and well distributed public key. Each time the repository is updated, the package file hashes are updated in the index and the final index hash is updated in the Release file, which is then signed. This chain of hashes, with the root signed, allows the consumer to authenticate the software they are about to install.

In the event that you are unable to sign a software release in some way, it is essential to revert to standard security practices. You will need to ensure that all communications are mutually authenticated - that means traffic to, from and between each distribution repository. In addition, you'll need to ensure that the storage used by the repository is properly secured, whether it's AWS S3 or otherwise.

Trusting a distribution network

When distributing software with a large or geographically disparate consumer base, it is common to copy the software to multiple locations or repositories to address scaling, availability, or performance issues. These copies are often referred to as mirrors. In some cases, especially when it comes to publicly consumed software, the servers hosting the mirrors are not under the control of the organization that produces the software. This is obviously a concern, and highlights the requirement for repo software to be authenticated against the author (not the repository owner).

Going back to the APT hash and signature scheme, we can see that we can, in fact, authenticate the Release file against the author by using its signature. This means that for each mirror we access, we can check the Release signature to validate that the mirror is in fact a faithful copy of the original version.

One might think that by signing the release file, the software can be distributed via unsecured mirrors safely. Furthermore, repositories are often hosted without TLS under the assumption that signing the release is sufficient to protect the distribution network. Unfortunately, both of these assertions are incorrect.

There are several classes of attacks that open up when connecting to an untrusted mirror, despite the fact that the artifact you get is ultimately signed. For example, a downgrade to an older (signed) version can be forced, as the artifact served will still be legitimate. Other attack vectors may include targeting the package management client itself. In order to protect your clients, always ensure that they connect to a secure distribution mirror.

The lack of TLS-protected repositories presents another vulnerability to software distribution. Attackers who are able to modify the unprotected response could perform the same attacks as an unauthorized mirror. Therefore, the best solution to this problem is to move package distribution to TLS-protected mechanisms. By adding TLS, clients can validate that they are actually connecting to a secure repository and that no tampering with the communication can occur.

Humans in the loop

With a secure pipeline designed, we can make conscious decisions about where humans are involved in the pipeline. By limiting human involvement to a few key points, the publishing pipeline remains secure while ensuring that hackers cannot leverage the automation in the pipeline to deliver malware.

The ability to validate code in the version control system is a clear place where humans are involved. Depending on the sensitivity of the project, requiring humans to check only signed commits provides confidence that the commit is authentic.

Once committed, humans do not need to be involved in the construction of software artifacts. These artifacts should ideally be produced automatically in a secure system. Humans should, however, be involved in the process of choosing the artifact that is ultimately distributed. This involvement could be implemented using various mechanisms: copying an artifact from the build database to the version database or marking a particular validation in the source control, for example. The mechanism by which humans certify a releasable binary does not matter much, as long as that mechanism is secure.

It is tempting, when building secure systems, to apply extreme measures to mitigate any conceivable threat, but the burden on humans should be weighed against the potential risk. In the case of widely distributed software, the private signing key should be well guarded, as the effort to rotate a compromised key would be extreme. Organizations releasing such software typically use "code signing ceremonies", where the signing key is stored on a hardware security module (HSM) and unlocked using multi-party authorization, to prevent theft of this highly sensitive key. For internal use only software, the effort to rotate a key may be reasonably less, so more lax security practices are reasonable. An organization may still prefer a code signing ceremony for particularly sensitive internal applications - a system that stores credit card details, for example.

Humans and code signing keys

Bit9 is a software security company that develops an application for whitelisting applications.

They have had many prestigious clients, from government agencies to Fortune 100 companies (Fortune magazine that ranks the top 100 companies based on revenue). In 2013, an attack on their corporate network recovered one of Bit9's private code signing keys, which was then used to sign and install malware on a handful of its customers. It is widely believed that this was done in order to bypass the strong security provided by the Bit9 software itself, and highlights the importance of securing code signing keys. If you have a high risk, as Bit9 did, it might be wise to use a code signing ceremony.

Trusting a body

Understanding what works in your infrastructure is important when designing a Zero Trust network. After all, how can you know what to expect on your network if you don't know what to expect on your hosts? A good understanding of the software (and versions) running in your data center will go a long way in detecting vulnerabilities and mitigating them.

Upgrade policy only

Software versions are important constructs for determining exactly what version of code you have and how old it is. Perhaps most importantly, they are widely used to determine what vulnerabilities one might be exposed to, given the version they run.

Vulnerability announcements/discoveries are usually associated with a version number (online service vulnerabilities being the exception) and usually include the version numbers in which the vulnerability has been fixed. With this in mind, we can see that it may be desirable to induce a version downgrade to expose a known vulnerability. This is an effective attack vector because the software that is forced to run is frequently authorized and approved, since it is a perfectly valid version, even if it is older.

If the software is designed for internal distribution, the distribution system may only serve the latest copy. This prevents a compromised or misconfigured system from extracting an older version that may contain a known vulnerability. It is also possible to apply this roll-forward mentality in hardware. Apple iOS uses a hardware security chip to validate software updates and ensure that only signed software built after the currently installed software can be loaded.

Authorized bodies

The importance of knowing what works is more nuanced than simply understanding which version was last deployed. Many workarounds occur, such as a host that has fallen out of the deployment system; one that was previously authorized but is now "rogue" by not receiving updates. In order to guard against cases like this, it is essential that running instances are authorized individually.

It is possible to use the techniques described in Chapter 4 to create a dynamic network policy for the purpose of authorizing application instances, but the network policy is often host/device oriented rather than application oriented. Instead, we can take advantage of something more application-centric in the pursuit of authorizing a running instance: secrets.

Most running applications require some sort of secret to do their job. This secret can manifest itself in many ways: an API key, an X509 certificate, or even message queue credentials are common examples. Applications must obtain the secret(s) in order to function, and furthermore, the secret must be valid. The validity of a secret (as obvious as it may seem) is the key to authorizing a running application, because with validation comes invalidation.

Attaching a lifetime to a secret is extremely effective in limiting its abuse. By creating a new secret for each instance deployed and attaching a lifetime to the secret, we can say that we know precisely what works, since we know precisely how many secrets we have generated, who we have given them to, and their lives. Allowing secrets to expire mitigates the impact of "rogue" instances by ensuring that they will not run indefinitely.

Of course, someone has to be responsible for generating and injecting these secrets at runtime, and this is no small responsibility. The system that bears this responsibility is ultimately the system that allows the instance to run. As such, it makes sense that this responsibility falls to the deployment system, as it already carries a similar responsibility.

Trusted third party in the authorization of proceedings

Rather than giving your deployment system direct access to secrets, it is possible to leverage a trusted third party, allowing the deployment system to instead assign rules dictating which secrets the running instance can access. The Hashicorp Vault, for example, has a feature called response return in which an authorized party can request that a secret be generated and stored for later retrieval. In the context of a deployment system, the deployment itself can contact Vault and direct the creation of secrets on behalf of authorized instances, injecting a unique token into the runtime that the application can use to retrieve the generated secrets. See Figure 7-6.
In such a system, the deployment service notifies the secret management service of impending changes, authorizing new application instances. During the actual deployment, the deployment service injects one or more keys, which the new instances use to identify themselves to the secret management system, which waits for their request. The secret management system then provides unique time-related credentials, returns them to the application, and continues to manage their life cycle.

It doesn't take much thought to realize the power of a system that can create and (eventually) recover secrets. With great power comes great responsibility. If allowing an autonomous system to generate and distribute secrets carries too much risk for your organization, you may want to consider including a human at this stage. Ideally, this would manifest as a human-approved deployment in which a TOTP or other authentication code is provided. This code will, in turn, be used to authorize the creation/extraction of secrets by the deployment system.

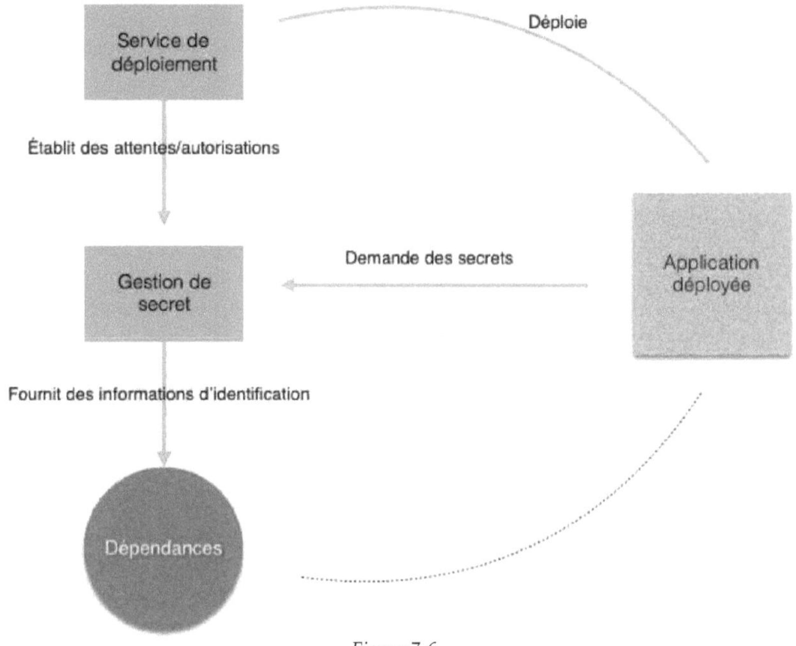

Figure 7-6

Security of execution

Having confidence that an application instance is authorized / sanctioned is only part of the concern. It is also necessary to validate that it can run safely throughout its lifecycle. We know how to deploy an application safely, and validate that its deployment is authorized, but will it remain an authorized and trusted deployment for its entire life?

Many vectors can compromise perfectly authorized application instances, and it is not surprising to learn that these are the most commonly used vectors. For example, it is generally easier to corrupt an existing government agent than to impersonate or attempt to become one. For this reason, people with outstanding debts are often denied security clearance. They may have full confidence when obtaining the clearance, but how corrupt are they likely to be if they are in debt? Can they be trusted in this case?

Secure Coding Practices

Most (all?) application-level vulnerabilities start with a latent bug, which an attacker can use to coerce the trusted application into performing an unwanted action. Fixing each bug in isolation will result in a game of whack-a-mole, where developers fix one security-impacting bug only to find two more. Really mitigating this exposure requires a shift in the mindset of application developers to secure coding practices.

Injection attacks, in which user-supplied data is designed to exploit a weakness in an application or associated system, typically occur when user data is not properly validated before being processed. This type of attack is mitigated by introducing multiple layers of defenses. Application libraries carefully build APIs that avoid trusting user-supplied data.

Database query libraries, for example, will provide APIs to allow the programmer to separate the static query from user-supplied variables. By establishing a clear separation between logic and data, the potential for injection attacks is greatly reduced.

Clear APIs can also support automated analysis of application software. Security-conscious organizations are increasingly using automated analysis tools against their source code to detect and warn application developers of insecure coding practices. These systems warn against the use of insecure APIs, for example, by highlighting database queries built using string concatenation instead of the API described above. Beyond warning about insecure APIs, application logic can be followed to identify missing checks. For example, these tools can confirm that every system transaction includes an authorization check, which mitigates vulnerabilities that allow hackers to reference data they should not have access to. These examples represent only a handful of the capabilities of code analysis tools.

Proactive identification of known vulnerabilities is useful, but some vulnerabilities are too subtle to be detected deterministically. As a result, another mitigation technique used is fuzzing. This practice sends random data to running applications to detect unexpected errors. These errors, when exposed, are often the kind of weaknesses that attackers use to gain a foothold in the system. Fuzzing can be run as part of a functional test suite early in the build pipeline, or even continuously against the production infrastructure.

There are entire books on secure coding practices, some of which depend on the type of application being created. Programmers need to familiarize themselves with the appropriate practices to improve the security of their applications. Many organizations choose to have security consultants inspect their applications and development practices to identify problems.

Insulation

Isolating deployed applications by limiting the set of resources they can access is important in a zero-trust network. Applications have traditionally been run in a shared environment, where a user's applications run in a runtime environment with very few constraints on how those applications can interact. This shared environment creates a great deal of risk if an application is compromised and presents similar challenges to the perimeter model.

Application isolation aims to limit the damage of a potentially compromised application by clearly defining the resources available to the application. Isolation will limit the capabilities and resources provided by the operating system:
- CPU time
- Memory access
- Network access - Filesystem access
- System calls

When implemented to the best of its ability, each application is given the least amount of access to complete its work. A well-constrained application that becomes compromised will quickly find that there is no additional leverage in the larger system. Therefore, by isolating applications, the potential damage from a compromised application is greatly reduced. In a multi-process environment (e.g., a server running multiple services), other still secure services are protected from attempts to move laterally on that system.

Application isolation can be accomplished using a number of different technologies:
- SELinux, AppArmor - BSD jails
- Virtualization/ containerization

- Apple's App Sandbox
- Windows' Isolated Applications

Isolation is generally considered to fall into two types: virtualization and shared kernel environments. Virtualization is often considered more secure because the application is contained in a virtual hardware environment, which is managed by a hypervisor outside of the virtual machine's runtime environment. Having a clear boundary between the hypervisor and the virtual machine creates the smaller surface of the two.

Shared kernel environments, such as those used in container or application policy systems, provide isolation guarantees, but not to the same degree as a fully virtualized system. A shared kernel runtime environment uses fewer resources to run the same set of applications and is therefore favored by cost-conscious organizations. As virtualization attempts to solve the resource efficiency problem, by providing more direct access to the underlying hardware, the security benefits of the virtualized environment begin to look more like the shared kernel environment. Depending on your threat model, you may choose not to share hardware.

Active monitoring

As with any production system, careful monitoring and logging is of the utmost importance and is especially critical in the context of security. Traditional security models focus their attention on external attack vectors. Zero Trust networks encourage the same level of rigor for internal activity. Early detection of an attack could mean the difference between complete compromise and prevention altogether.

In addition to general logging of security events across the infrastructure, such as unsuccessful or successful connections, which is considered passive monitoring, there is also an entire class of active monitoring. For example, the fuzzing scans we've already discussed can take time to reveal new vulnerabilities - perhaps longer than you'd like. An active monitoring strategy calls for scans to be directed against production as well, on an ongoing basis.

Don't do this in production!
Sometimes the desire to take certain steps in production may be resisted for fear of impacting the availability or stability of the overall system. Security scans frequently fall into this bucket. In reality, while a security scan may destabilize your system, there is a larger underlying problem, which may even be a vulnerability in itself. Rather than avoiding potentially dangerous scans in production, ask them why they might be risky, and work to ensure that they can be safely managed by resolving the system failures that contribute to the problem.

Of course, fuzzing is just one example. Automated analysis can be a useful tool for ensuring consistent behavior in a system. For example, a database of anticipated listening services could be compared to an automated scan of actual listening services so that discrepancies can be corrected. However, not all scanning will result in such clear action. Scanning installed software, for example, will typically be used to prioritize upgrades based on the threats a network is exposed to or expects to see.

Effective system analysis requires several types of scanners, each of which inspects the system in a slightly different way:
- Fuzzing (afl-fuzz)

- Injection scanning (sqlmap)
- Network port scanning (nmap)
- Common vulnerability scanning (nessus)

So, what do you do when all this monitoring uncovers something? The answer usually depends on the strength of the signal. Traditionally, suspicious (but not critical) events are dumped into reports and reviewed periodically. This practice is by far the least effective, as it can lead to fatigue, with reports going unnoticed for weeks. Alternatively, important events can page a human for active investigation. These events have a strong enough signal to warrant waking someone up. In most cases, this is the strongest line of defense.

Application monitoring applications

A novel idea in the context of application security monitoring is the idea that applications participating in a single cluster or service can actively monitor the health of their peers and gain consensus with others about their sanity. This can manifest itself in the form of TPM citations, behavioral analysis, and everything in between. By allowing applications to monitor each other, you get a high signal-to-noise ratio while spreading the responsibility across the infrastructure. This approach most effectively protects against side-channel attacks, or attacks enabled by multi-tenancy, because these vectors are less likely to be shared across the cluster.

In highly automated environments, a third option opens up: active response. Strong signals that "something is wrong" can trigger automated actions in the infrastructure. This can mean revoking keys belonging to the suspect instance, booting it from cluster membership, or even signaling to the data center management software that the instance should be moved offline and isolated for forensics.

Of course, as with all high-level automation, a lot of damage can be done very quickly by using active responses. It is possible to introduce denial of service attacks with such mechanisms, or perhaps more likely, to stop a service due to operator error. When designing active response systems, it is important to implement a number of security features. For example, an active response that ejects a host from a cluster should not be triggered if the cluster size is dangerously small. Being careful about building active response limitations such as this helps ensure the sanity of the active response process itself.

Summary

This chapter focuses on how applications in a Zero Trust network are secured. It may seem counterintuitive that a zero trust network should be concerned with application security. After all, the network is untrusted, hence the presence of untrusted applications on the network. However, while the network functions to detect and identify malicious application activity, this goal is made impossible if deployed applications are not properly validated before being allowed to run. Therefore, the majority of this chapter has focused on how to safely develop, create, and deploy applications in a Zero Trust network and then monitor the running instances to ensure that they remain trusted.

The chapter introduced the concept of a trusted application pipeline, which is the mechanism by which software written by trusted developers is transformed into embedded applications that are then deployed in the infrastructure. This pipeline is a very valuable target for potential attackers, so it deserves special attention. We looked at secure source code hosting practices, best practices for transforming source code into trusted artifacts, and the secure selection and distribution of these artifacts to downstream consumers. The application pipeline can be visualized as a series of immutable transformations on the input from the pipeline. We therefore explored how to achieve the goals of this pipeline without introducing too much friction into the process.

Human attention is a scarce but important resource in a secure system. With the ever-increasing rate of software releases, it is important to carefully consider when humans are best introduced into the process. We discussed where to put humans in the loop to ensure the pipeline remains secure.

Once applications are built, the process of securing their continued execution in a production environment shifts a bit. In the future, older trusted applications may become untrusted as vulnerabilities are discovered. So we discussed the importance of an upgrade-only policy at application runtime. Secret management is often a difficult task for security engineers, where changing credentials is often very tedious. With a smooth credential provisioning process, however, a new opportunity arises to rotate credentials frequently, using the credentialing process itself as a mechanism to ensure that only authorized applications continue to run in a production environment.

We ended the chapter with a section on good application security hygiene. Learning secure coding practices, deploying applications in isolated environments, and aggressively monitoring them is the final step in a reliable production environment.

With all the components of a zero-trust network explored, the next chapter focuses on how network communication is itself secure.

Chapter 8:
Trust the traffic

Authentication and authorization of network flows is a critical aspect of a zero-trust network. In this chapter, we'll discuss how encryption fits into the picture, how to bootstrap trust into the flow through a secure introduction, and where these security protocols best fit into your network.

Zero trust is not a complete departure from everything we know. Traditional network filtering still plays an important role in zero-trust networks, although its application is not traditional. We will explore the role that filtering plays in these networks toward the end of this chapter.

Encryption versus authentication

Encryption and authenticity often go hand in hand, but serve distinct purposes. Encryption ensures confidentiality - the promise that only the recipient can read the data you are sending. Authentication allows a receiver to validate that the message was sent by the thing it claims to be.

Authentication comes with another interesting property. To ensure the authenticity of a message, you must be able to validate the sender and not alter the message. Referred to as integrity, this is an essential property of message authentication.

Encryption is possible without authentication, although this is considered bad security practice. Without sender validation, an attacker is free to forge messages, possibly replaying previous "good" messages. An attacker could change the ciphertext, and the receiver would have no way of knowing this. There are a number of vectors opened up by omitting authentication, so the recommendation is pretty much the same in all areas: use it.

Authenticity without encryption?

Authenticity of messages is a stated requirement of a zero-trust network, and it is not possible to create one without it. But what about encryption?
Encryption provides privacy, but it can also be an occasional nuisance. Troubleshooting becomes more difficult when you can't read packet captures without a complicated decryption process. Intrusion detection becomes difficult or impossible if network traffic cannot be inspected. There are, in fact, legitimate reasons to avoid encryption.

That said, be absolutely certain that you don't care about data privacy if you choose not to use encryption.

Although keeping data unencrypted is convenient for administrators, it is never legitimate for the data to be truly confidential. For example, consider the scenario shown in Figure 8-1.

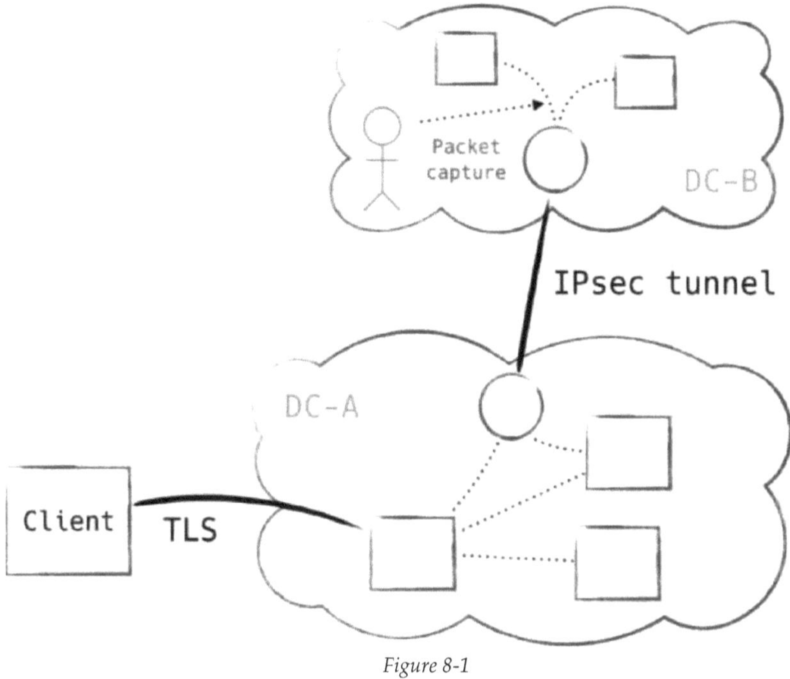

Figure 8-1

This is an extremely common architecture. Note that it only encrypts traffic in certain areas, leaving the rest open (perhaps for the benefit of system administrators). However, this data clearly requires privacy, as it is encrypted in transit between sites.

This is a direct contradiction of the zero-trust architecture, as it creates privileged areas in the network. Thus, citing good reasons not to encrypt traffic is a very slippery slope. In practice, systems that don't really need privacy are rare.

In addition to all this, authentication is always required. There are few network protocols that provide strong authentication but not encryption, and all the transport protocols we discuss in this book provide authentication as well as encryption. If you look at it this way, encryption is achieved "for free", leaving few good reasons to exclude it.

Starting the trust: the first package

The first packet in a flow is often expensive. Depending on the type of connection, or the lifecycle point of the device, this packet can carry very little trust.

We usually know what to expect in the data center, but in customer-facing systems, it's anyone's guess. These systems need to be widely accessible, which greatly increases the risk. We can use protocols such as mutually authenticated TLS to authenticate the device before it is allowed to access the service; however, the attack surface in this scenario is still considerable and the resources are also publicly detectable.

So how do you allow only trusted connections, silently dropping all others, without responding to a single unauthenticated packet? This is known as the first packet problem, and it is mitigated by a method called pre-authentication (Figure 8-2).

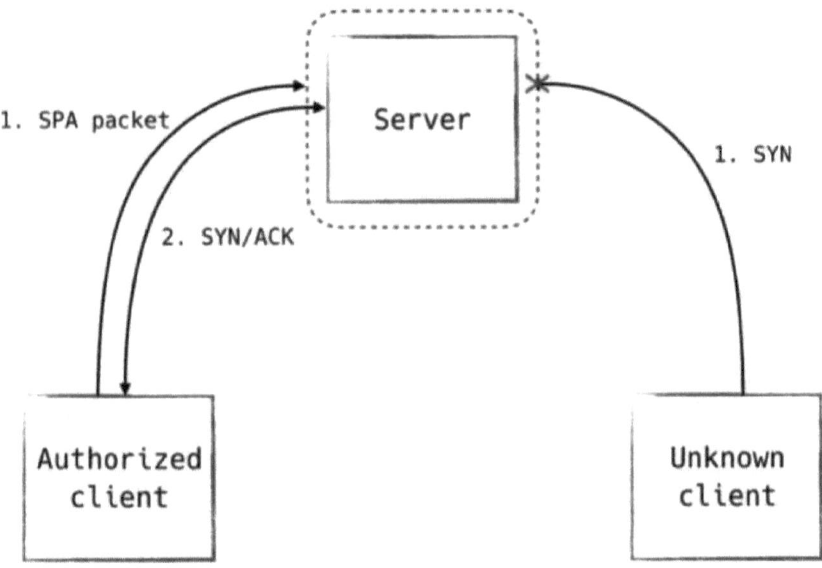

Figure 8-2

Pre-authentication can be thought of as authorizing an authentication request by setting an expectation for it. It is often accomplished by encrypting and/or signing a small piece of data and sending it to the resource as a UDP packet. Using UDP for pre-authentication is important because UDP packets do not receive a response by default. This property allows us to "hide", only exposing ourselves once we passively receive an encrypted packet with the correct key.

When passively receiving a properly encrypted pre-authentication packet, we know that we can expect the sender to start authenticating with us, and we can drill granular firewall holes allowing the sender to talk to our TLS server. This pre-authentication mode of operation is also called Single Packet Authorization (SPA).

SPA is not a fully compliant device authentication protocol. It simply helps to mitigate the first packet problem. Without minimizing the importance of the properties we get by using pre-authentication, it should not be replaced by a more robust mutual authentication protocol such as TLS or IKE.

fwknop

fwknop is a popular open source SPA implementation. It supports a wide variety of operating systems and integrates directly with host firewalls to coordinate the creation of short-lived, limited scope exceptions.

Short-term exceptions
When fwknop receives a valid SPA packet, its contents are decrypted and inspected. The

decrypted payload includes the protocol and port numbers to which the sender is requesting access. fwknop uses this to create firewall rules allowing the sender's traffic to those particular ports - rules that are removed after a configurable period of time. The default is 30 seconds, but in practice you only need a few seconds.

Payload SPA
The SPA implementation of fwknop has seven mandatory and three optional fields included in its payload. These include a username, the access request itself (which port, etc.), a timestamp and a checksum: -16 bytes of random data
- Local username
- Localt

imestamp
- fwknop version
- SPA message type
- Access request
- SPA message digest (SHA-256 by default)

Once the client has generated the payload, it is encrypted, an optional HMAC is added and the SPA packet is formed and transmitted.

Payload encryption

Two encryption modes are supported: AES and GnuPG. The former being symmetric and the latter being asymmetric, two options are offered to meet multiple use cases and preferences.

Personal applications or small installations may prefer AES because they do not require any GnuPG tools. AES is also more efficient in terms of data volume and computational overhead. It does have some drawbacks, however, almost all of which stem from the fact that it is a symmetric algorithm.

Symmetric encryption comes with difficult key distribution problems, and beyond a certain scale, these challenges can become untenable. Using the GnuPG encryption mode solves most of these problems and is the recommended mode of operation, although it performs worse than its counterpart.

HMAC

fwknop can be configured to add an HMAC at the end of its payload.

A hashed message authentication code (HMAC) prevents forgery by ensuring that the message is authentic. This is important because otherwise an attacker could arbitrarily modify the ciphertext, and the receiver would be forced to process it.

You may have noticed that there is a message digest that is calculated and stored with the plain text. This digest helps mitigate attacks in which the ciphertext is modified, but is also not ideal, as this method (known as authenticate-then-encrypt or AtE) is vulnerable to a few niche classes of attacks. Adding an HMAC to the cipher load prevents these attacks from being effective.

In addition, decryption routines are generally much more complex than HMAC routines, which means they are more likely to suffer from a vulnerability. Applying an HMAC to the ciphertext allows the receiver to perform a light integrity check, which ensures that we are only sending trusted data to the decryption routines.

It is strongly recommended to configure fwknop to use HMAC.

A brief introduction to network models

Network stacks have many different responsibilities in the transmission of data over a network. As such, it would be easy for a network stack to become a mess of code. Therefore, the industry has long since decided to make the effort to clearly define a set of standardized layers in a network stack. Each layer is responsible for a portion of the work of transmitting data over the wire. The lower layers provide functionality and guarantee higher layers in the stack.

Building these layers is not only useful for organizing code. These layer definitions are often used to describe where the new technology works in the stack.

For example, you may have heard of a Layer 7 or Layer 4 load balancer. A load balancer distributes the traffic load across a set of backend machines, but the layer at which it operates greatly determines its capabilities. A layer 7 load balancer, for example, can make traffic routing decisions based on the details of an HTTP request such as the requested path or a particular header. HTTP operates at layer 7, so this data is available for inspection. In contrast, a Layer 4 load balancer does not consider Layer 7 data and so can only forward traffic based on simpler connection details, such as the source IP address and port.

There are many different network models. Most of these models can be roughly mapped to equivalents in other network models, but sometimes the boundaries can be a bit blurry. For this book, we will focus only on two network models: the OSI network model and the TCP/IP network model. Understanding the boundaries of these two models will help in later discussions of where zero-trust responsibilities should be addressed in the network model.

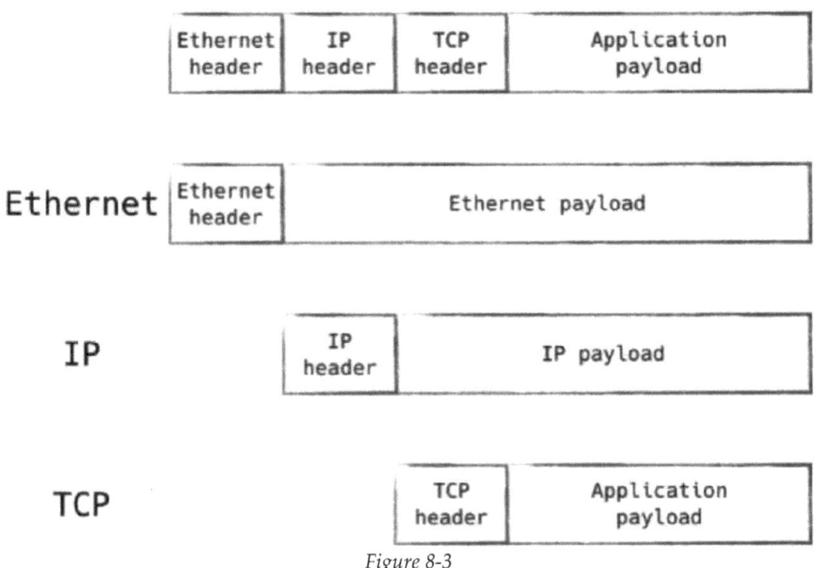

Figure 8-3

Network layers, visually

The idea of a layer may be strange at first, although a simplistic way to understand the concept is to compare them to Russian dolls. Each layer typically contains the next, encapsulated by it in a section known as the payload (Figure 8-3).

OSI network model

The OSI network model was published in 1984 after being merged from two separate documents started several years earlier. The model is published by two separate standards bodies: the International Organization for Standardization (ISO) published ISO 7498, while the Telecommunications Standardization Sector of the International Telecommunication Union (ITU-T) published X. 200.

The model itself is derived from the experiences of building several networks at the time, ARPANET being the best known. The model defines seven distinct layers (explained in the following sections), each of which has a share of the responsibilities for data transmission.

Layer 1 - Physical layer

The physical layer is defined as the interface between a network device and the physical medium over which network transmission takes place. This can include such things as pin layout, line impedance, voltage and frequency. The physical layer (sometimes called PHY) parameters depend on the type of media used. Twisted pair, coaxial cabling and radio waves are examples of media commonly used today.

Layer 2 - Data link layer

The data link layer is responsible for the transmission of data on the physical layer. This layer only considers the transmission of data between directly connected nodes. There is no concept of transmission between interconnected networks. Ethernet (802.3) is the best known protocol operating on this layer.

Layer 3 - Network layer

The network layer is responsible for the transmission of data packets between two interconnected nodes. In this layer, packets may need to traverse several layer 2 segments to reach their destination, which includes concepts for routing data to its destination by inspecting a destination address. IP is often said to work at this layer, but the boundaries can be a bit fuzzy, as we'll see later.

Layer 4 - Transport layer

The transport layer builds on the simple packet transmission capabilities of Layer 3, usually as an intermediate protocol designed to augment Layer 3 with many desirable services:

- Stateful connections
- Multiplexing
- Ordered delivery
- Flow control -
  Broadcasting

These services may look like the services that a protocol like TCP provides. In fact, TCP is a Layer 4 protocol; however, in a similar way to IP, this association can be a bit awkward.

Not all of these services need to be provided by a protocol operating at this level. UDP, for example, is a layer 4 protocol that provides only one of these services (multiplexing). It remains a layer 4 protocol because it is an intermediate protocol that is directly encapsulated by layer 3.

Layer 5 - Session layer
The session layer is not commonly discussed in most networks. This layer provides an additional layer of state over connections, allowing communication to be resumed and communicated through an intermediary. Several VPN (PPTP, L2TP) and proxy (SOCKS) protocols operate at this layer.

Layer 6 - Presentation layer
The presentation layer is the layer that application developers will interact with most often. This layer is responsible for managing the translation between application data (often represented as structural data) and transmissible data streams. In addition to this serialization responsibility, this layer is often responsible for crosscutting issues such as encryption and compression. TLS is a well-known protocol operating at this layer, although it operates at layer 6 only after the session has been established (which happens at layer 5 - the process of moving from a lower to a higher layer is sometimes called).

Layer 7 - Application layer
The application layer is the highest layer of the OSI model. This layer provides the high-level communication protocols that an application uses to communicate over the network. Some common protocols at this layer are DNS, HTTP and SSH.

TCP/IP network model

The TCP/IP network model is another important network model. This model deals with the most common protocols found on the internet today.

Unlike the OSI model, the TCP/IP model does not attempt to define strict layers with clear boundaries. In fact, RFC 3439, which documents the "philosophical guidelines" that Internet architects use has a section entitled "Layering Considered Harmful". Yet the model is said to define the following rough layers, from lowest to highest:
-   link layer

- internet layer - Transport layer - Application layer
These layers can be roughly mapped to the OSI model, but the mappings are only the best effort. The application layer roughly covers layers 5-7 in the OSI model. The transport layer corresponds roughly to layer 4, although the introduction of the port concept gives it some characteristics of layer 5. Similarly, the Internet layer is generally associated with layer 3. The abstraction is leaky, however, because higher-level protocols such as ICMP (which are transmitted over IP) are concerned with the details of routing traffic over the Internet.

Where should Zero Trust be in the network model?

With a better understanding of network layer models, we can now examine where to best apply zero trust checks in the network stack.

There are two predominant network security suites: TLS and IPsec. TLS (Transport Layer Security, to which SSL is a predecessor) is the more common of the two. Many application layer protocols support TLS to secure traffic. IPsec is an alternative protocol, more commonly used to secure things like VPNs.

Despite the fact that "transport" is in its name, TLS does not reside in the transport layer of the TCP/IP model. It resides in the application layer (somewhere between layers 5 and 6 of the OSI model) and, as such, is largely an application problem.

TLS as an infrastructure concern

Perimeter networks often remove TLS from applications, shifting responsibility for the application to the infrastructure. In this mode, TLS is "terminated" by a dedicated device on the perimeter, passing decrypted traffic to a backend service. While this mode of operation is not possible in a zero-trust network, there are still a handful of strategies for deploying TLS as an infrastructure concern while conforming to the zero-trust model. More on this later.

In contrast, IPsec is generally considered to be part of the Internet layer in the TCP/IP model (layer 3 or 4 in the OSI model, depending on the interpretation). Further down the stack, IPsec is usually implemented in the kernel of a host. IPsec was developed for the IPv6 specification. It was originally a requirement for IPv6, but was eventually downgraded to recommended status.

With two alternatives for securing the transport network, the question becomes, is one preferred over the other? The goal of Zero Trust is secure communication for all traffic. The best way to achieve this goal is to create systems that provide secure communication by default.

IPsec, being a low-level service, is well positioned to provide this service.

By using IPsec, host-to-host communication can be permanently secured. Embedded in the core of the network stack, IPsec can be configured to only allow packets to be transmitted once a secure communication channel has been established. In addition, the receiver side can be configured to only process packets that have been sent securely. In this system, we have essentially created a "secure virtual wire" between two hosts over which only secure traffic can flow. This is a huge advantage over traditional security initiatives that add secure communication one application at a time.

Simply securing communications between two devices is not enough to create a zero-trust network. We need to ensure that each individual network flow is authorized. There are several options for meeting this need: - IPsec can use a single security association (SA) per application (see RFC

4301, section 4.4.1.1). Only authorized flows are then allowed to build these security policies.
- Filtering systems (software firewalls) can be layered over IPsec. We will discuss the role of filtering in zero trust later in this chapter.
- Application-level authorization should be used to ensure that communications are authorized. This could use standard authorization techniques, such as access tokens or X.509 certificates, while delegating strong encryption and authentication responsibilities to the IPsec stack.
- For a true "belt and braces" system, mutually authenticated TLS could be layered on top of the existing IPsec layer. This defense-in-depth approach provides two layers of encryption (TLS and IPsec), protecting the communication if one of them were compromised, at the expense of complexity and increased cost.

Split client and server

While IPsec has a number of beneficial properties, its lack of popularity presents real obstacles to its use in systems today. The problems we will see can be divided into three areas:
- Network support issues
- Device support issues
- Application support issues

Network support issues

Network support may hinder the use of IPsec in the wild. IPsec introduces several new protocols, two of which (ESP and AH) are new IP protocols. While these protocols are fully supported in simple LANs, on some networks, transmission of these packets can be very difficult. This can be due to misconfigured firewalls, NAT traversal, or deliberate configuration of routers to prevent traffic from flowing. For example, Amazon Web Services, a large public cloud provider, does not allow ESP or AH traffic to be transmitted over its networks. Public hotspots, such as those found in businesses or libraries, often have uneven support for IPsec traffic.

To mitigate these problems, IPsec includes support for encapsulating traffic in a UDP frame (see Figure 8-4). This encapsulation allows an inhospitable network to transmit traffic, but adds additional complexity to the system.

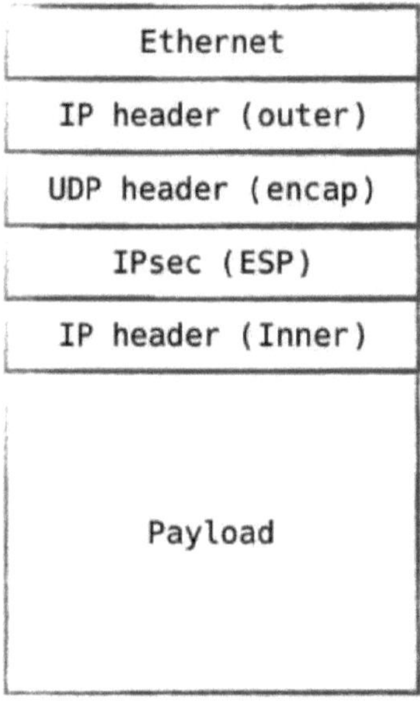

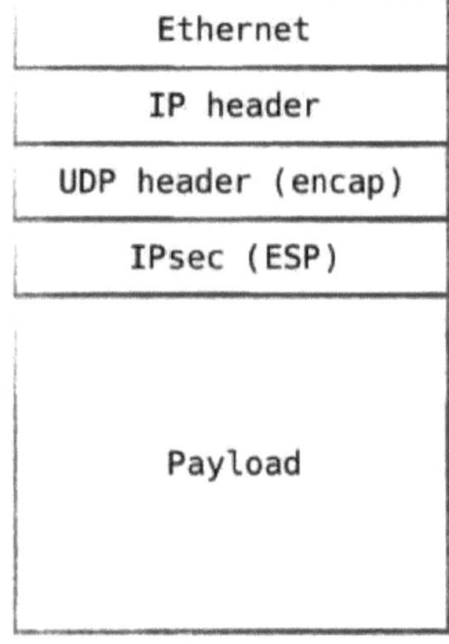

Figure 8-4

Device support issues

Device support can also be an important factor in deploying an IPsec protected network. The IPsec standard is complex, with many configuration options and cipher suites. Both hosts in the relationship must agree to a common protocol and cipher suite before communication can flow.

Cipher suites in particular often need to be adjusted as compromises are revealed. Finding that a stronger cipher suite has not been implemented is a real problem in IPsec systems. To be fair, TLS has to deal with these same issues; but due to the nature of IPsec's implementation in the core system, progress on new protocols and cipher suites is naturally slower.

IPsec also requires active configuration of devices in the relationship. In a client/server system with varying device capabilities, configuring client devices can be quite difficult. Desktop operating systems can usually be configured to support the less popular protocol. However, mobile operating systems are less likely to fully support IPsec in a manner consistent with the zero-trust model.

Application support issues

IPsec places additional requirements on system configuration than typical TLS-based security. A system wishing to use IPsec must configure the IPsec policy, enable kernel support for the desired cipher suites, and run an IKE daemon to facilitate negotiation of IPsec security associations. Compared to a library-based approach for TLS, this additional complexity can be daunting. This is doubly true when many applications already have built-in TLS support, which seems to offer a turnkey solution for network security.

It should be noted that while the library approach seems more attractive at first glance, in practice it has some hidden complexity. As a library, applications must expose configuration controls to the TLS library. Applications often support the more common TLS server, but neglect to expose the configuration to present a client certificate required to create a mutually authenticated TLS connection. In addition, system administrators may need to adjust the configuration in response to a newly discovered vulnerability. With a large number of applications, finding the application-specific configuration that needs to be adjusted can hinder the deployment of a critical patch.

The web browser is frequently the common access point to organizational systems. Its support for modern TLS is generally very good (assuming organizations stay current on the latest browser versions). This common access point mitigates the configuration problem, as there are a small number of target applications that need to be adjusted.

On the server side, many organizations are moving to a model where network communication is secured via a local daemon. This approach centralizes the configuration in a single application and allows the system administrator to provide a basic layer of network security. In some ways, it is very similar to the IPsec model, but implemented using TLS instead.

A pragmatic approach

Considering all the advantages and disadvantages of both approaches, a pragmatic solution seems to be available for system administrators.

For client/server interactions, the mutually authenticated TLS protocol seems to be the most reasonable approach for network security. This approach typically involves configuring a browser to present client certificates to server-side access proxies that ensure the connection is authenticated and authorized. Of course, this limits the use of zero trust to browser-based applications.

For server/server interactions, IPsec seems more accessible. The server farm is generally under a more controlled configuration and the network environment is more familiar. For networks that do not support IPsec, UDP encapsulation can be used to avoid network transit issues.

Microsoft Server Isolation

For environments that integrate Microsoft Windows with Active Directory, a feature called server isolation is of particular interest. By leveraging Windows firewall, network policy and group policy, server isolation provides a framework through which IPsec configuration can be automated. In addition, server isolation can be linked to Active Directory security groups, enabling precise access control, supported by strong IPsec authentication.

While the complications surrounding IPsec transit over public networks still exist, server isolation is perhaps the most pragmatic approach to achieving zero-trust semantics in a Windows environment.

Since IPv6 includes IPsec, the author hopes that it will become a more viable solution for both types of network communication as the network is adopted.

The protocols

We learned about TLS and IPsec mutually authenticated in the previous section, as well as when you might use one over the other. In this section, we will discuss both protocols in detail. It is very important to understand the inner workings of these protocols as you deploy them, as they contain many configuration controls. Both are inherently complicated, and insecure configurations are common.

IKE/IPsec

Internet Key Exchange (IKE) is a protocol that runs the authentication and key exchange components of IPsec. It is typically implemented as a daemon and uses a pre-shared key or X.509 certificate to authenticate a peer and create a secure session. In this secure session, another key exchange is performed. The results of this second key exchange are then used to establish an IPsec security association, whose parameters are used for bulk data transfer. Let's take a closer look.

IKEV1 versus IKEV2

There are two versions of IKE and most software suites support both. For all new deployments, it is strongly recommended to use IKEv2. It is both more flexible and more reliable than its predecessor, which was overly complicated and underperforming. For the purposes of this book, we will talk exclusively about IKEv2.

IKE and IPsec

There is frequent confusion about the relationship between IKE and IPsec. The reality is that IPsec is not a single protocol; it is a collection of protocols. IKE is often considered part of the IPsec protocol suite, although its design makes it complementary to a main component. IKE can be considered the control plane of IPsec. It handles session negotiation and authentication, using the results of negotiation to configure endpoints with session keys and encryption algorithms.

Since the core IPsec protocols are built into the IP stack, IPsec implementations are usually found in the kernel. Because key exchange is a relatively complex mechanism, IKE is implemented as a user-space daemon. The kernel contains the state defining the active IPsec security associations and the traffic selectors defining the packets to which the IPsec policy should be applied. The IKE daemon handles everything else, including negotiating the IPsec security association (SA) itself (which is then installed in the kernel for use).

Authentication information

IKEv2 supports pre-shared keys and X.509 public/private key pairs. In addition, it supports the Extensible Authentication Protocol (EAP). Support for EAP means that IKEv2 supports a multitude of other authentication methods (including support for multi-factor authentication) on a per-proxy basis. However, we will avoid analyzing EAP directly, as the ecosystem is very large.

It goes without saying that X.509 certificates are the preferred authentication method for IKE. While pre-shared keys are supported, we strongly recommend that you do not use them. They present major distribution and generation challenges, but more importantly, they are for humans to remember.

X.509 certificates are not for humans. They are for devices. They provide not only proof of trust, but also signed metadata and a way to strongly encrypt data using one's identity. These are powerful properties, and the reason why certificates are the undisputed champions of device authentication information.

IKE SA_INIT and AUTH

All IKEv2 exchanges begin with a pair of packets named IKE_SA_INIT. This initial exchange handles cryptographic suite selection, as well as a Diffie-Hellman exchange. The Diffie-Hellman key exchange provides a method for two systems to negotiate a session key without ever transmitting it.

The resulting session key is used to encrypt the fields in the next message pair: the IKE_AUTH packets. In this step, the endpoints exchange certificates and generate what is called a CHILD_SA. CHILD_SA contains the IPsec parameters for a security association between the two endpoints, and the IKE daemon then programs these parameters into the kernel. From this point on, the kernel will encrypt all traffic corresponding to the selectors.

Selection of the cipher suite

The choice of encryption with IPsec is slightly less trivial than TLS. This is because IPsec is implemented in the kernel, making encryption support a bit more stringent than if it were just software. Therefore, a wide variety of devices and operating system versions will complicate IPsec deployments.

RFC 6379 describes the so-called cryptographic suite, Suite B. It was written by the US National Security Agency and is (at the time of writing) a widely accepted standard when it comes to selecting IPsec cipher suites.

Like TLS, IKE cipher suites include algorithms for key exchange, block cipher, and integrity. Unlike TLS, it does not include authentication, as IKE takes care of that outside of cipher suite selection.

RFC 6379 is quite prescriptive regarding these choices. All of the suites defined in Suite B take advantage of the different strengths of the AES encryption algorithm and the ECDH key agreement protocol. They take advantage of GCM and SHA for integrity. For most use cases, Suite B is recommended.

There are several cases in which the B-Suite may not be appropriate. The first is that not all IPsec implementations support elliptic curve cryptography, which is mandatory. The second is the security of the popularized elliptic curve implementation, as many believe that state actors have interfered with them to subvert the security they aim to provide.

In either case, an equivalent DH is recommended as a good alternative.

IPsec Security Associations

IPsec security associations (SAs) are the end result of an IKE negotiation and describe what is sometimes called a "relationship" with the remote endpoint.

They are unidirectional, so for a relationship between two endpoints, you will normally find two SAs (incoming and outgoing).

An IPsec SA is uniquely identified by an SPI (Security Parameter Index, not to be confused with an IKE SPI) and has a limited lifetime. As traffic traverses the IP stack, the kernel finds packets corresponding to the selector(s) and checks to see if there is an active security association for the selector in question. If there is an entry, the kernel encrypts the packet according to the parameters defined in the SA, and forwards it. If there is no entry, the kernel will tell the IKE daemon to negotiate one.

An IPsec AS has four distinct states in its life cycle: larval, mature, dying and dead.

A larval AS is one that is still being negotiated by the IKE daemon and has only part of its state installed. Once negotiation is complete, the SA transitions to the mature state, in which it begins to encrypt traffic. As the SA approaches the end of its lifetime, a new SA is negotiated and installed with the same policy. The original AS goes into a dead state and all relevant traffic switches to the new AS. After a period of time, the old AS expires and is marked as dead.

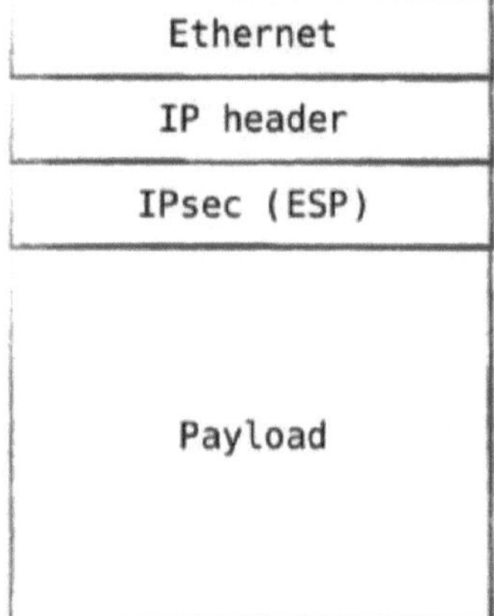

Figure 8-5

IPsec tunnel mode versus transport mode

IPsec supports two modes of operation, tunnel mode and transport mode (Figure 8-5).

Tunnel mode is by far the most widely deployed variant.

When IPsec operates in tunnel mode, an SA is formed with the remote endpoint which is used to encapsulate the IP packets and secure them en route to the endpoint. This encapsulation covers the entire IP packet, including the IP header. This means that in tunnel mode, the IPsec endpoint may be different from the endpoint to which the IP traffic is destined, as a new IP header will be exposed once the protected traffic is decompressed.

This is why it is called tunnel mode. It is frequently used in VPNs, where one wishes to establish a secure connection with a remote network, allowing administrators to channel traffic destined for that network through the secure channel. This brings an interesting realization but in the world of zero-trust networks: tunnel mode, by its very nature, strongly implies that traffic will become unprotected at some point. Security is provided between the sender and a network intermediary, but after that all bets are off. The author's opinion is that, for this reason, the use of tunnel mode contradicts the zero-trust architecture.

On the other hand, the transport mode offers almost identical security guarantees, just minus the tunnel part. Instead of encapsulating an entire IP packet, it encapsulates only the IP payload. This is useful for direct host-to-host IP communication. Rather than establishing a security association with an intermediate network device, the transport mode establishes a security association directly with the endpoint to which the traffic is addressed, thus ensuring that security is enforced end-to-end. This property allows the transport mode to fit seamlessly into the zero trust model.

While transport mode is the obvious choice for a complete zero trust data center architecture, it is important to remain realistic. Zero trust migrations are difficult and IPsec tunnel mode is still a tool that can be leveraged along the journey to a seamless zero trust architecture.

IKE / IPsec for device authentication

When it comes to device security in a zero-trust network, we're looking to provide not only authentication for the device, but also transport security from device to device. This is exactly what IPsec is designed to do, and why it may be the best protocol for the job.

Because IPsec is implemented directly on IP, it can handle most applications, not just TCP or UDP. Also, since it is implemented in the kernel, protected applications do not need to know the underlying security. They simply work as they normally would, and the traffic is encrypted for free.

This encryption and authenticity may come "free" from the application's perspective, but it's certainly not the case for the device! As you can see, IPsec configuration is non-trivial, and managing the multitude of policies can be difficult (or impossible without automation).

Another consideration is the support of IPsec as a network protocol. Not all public networks (e.g., coffee shops) support IPsec and may even actively block it. The difficulty of configuration and the lack of universal support make IPsec less desirable for client-side Zero Trust networks. However, these pain points generally do not exist inside the data center, where IPsec remains a competitor in terms of device security protocols.

TLS mutually authenticated

Commonly referred to by the name of its predecessor, Transport Layer Security (TLS) is the most commonly used protocol for securing Web traffic. It is a mature and well-understood protocol, widely deployed and supported, and is already recognized for some of the most sensitive tasks, such as banking transactions. That's the "S" in HTTPS.

When TLS is used to secure Web sessions, the client validates that the server certificate is valid, but the server rarely validates the client. In fact, the client rarely presents a certificate! The "mutual" prefix for TLS is intended to designate a TLS configuration in which client certificate validation is required (and thus mutually authenticated).

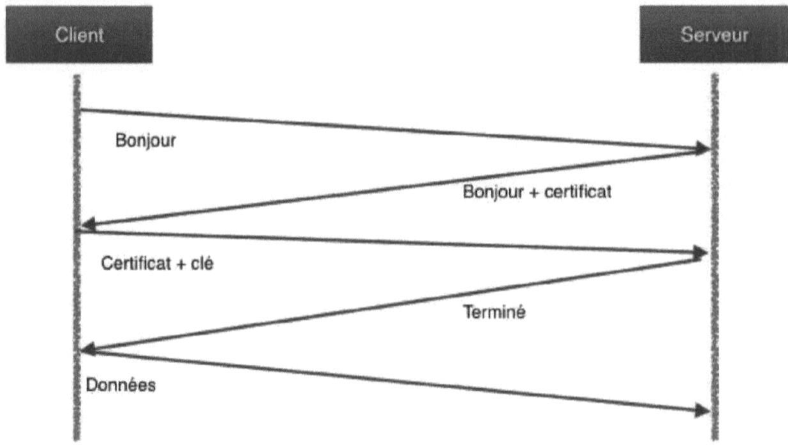

Figure 8-6

While a lack of client authentication may be acceptable for services that are published to the general public, it is not acceptable for any other use case. Mutual authentication is a requirement for zero-trust security protocols, and TLS is no exception.

The basics of a TLS handshake are fairly simple, as shown in Figure 8-6. A client initiates the session with a ClientHello message sent to the server, which includes a compatibility list for such things as cipher suites and compression methods. The server chooses parameters from the compatibility list and responds with a ServerHello defining the selections made, followed by the server's X.509 certificate. It also requests the client's certificate at this time.

The client then generates a secret key and uses the server's public key to encrypt it. It sends the server this encrypted secret key, along with its client certificate, and a small proof that it is in fact the owner of that certificate. The secret key generated by the client is eventually used to derive several additional keys, including one that acts as a symmetric session key. So, once the client has sent these details, it has enough information to set up its side of the encrypted session. It signals the server to switch to session encryption, the server validates the client, sends a similar message back and the session is fully upgraded.

Negotiation and selection of cipher suites

TLS supports many types of authentication and encryption. A cipher suite is a named combination of these components. There are four main components in a TLS cipher suite:
- key exchange
- authentication
- bulk encryption
- message authenticity

Choosing the right set of supported cipher suites is important to ensure the security of your TLS deployments. Many cipher suites are known to be weak. At the same time, the strongest cipher suites are poorly supported by clients in the wild.

Who can say

During TLS negotiation, the client presents its list of supported cipher suites in order of preference. The server can choose one from this list, assuming there is a shared medium, in which case the session will fail to establish. While the client communicates its encryption preferences to the server, it is ultimately the server that is allowed to choose. This is important because it preserves the client/server, consumer/operator relationship.

With this, overall system security is limited to the strongest negotiable cipher suite of the weakest client. Historically, many online resources support weak cipher suites in order to maintain backward compatibility with older clients.

Knowing this, there have been numerous attacks against cipher suite negotiation, including backtracking attacks that allow an attacker to actively weaken the encryption algorithm used by a client.

Therefore, it is recommended that servers support only the strongest set of cipher suites that is reasonable. In the case of data center deployments, this list may be limited to a few approved suites, as there is strict control over the "clients". However, this is not always reasonable for real client deployments.

Negotiation as a weakness

Cipher-suite negotiation is, for the reasons given, considered an anti-pattern in modern cryptographic protocols. New protocols and frameworks such as Noise aim to eliminate protocol negotiation. Work in this area is very active at the time of writing, and the author looks forward to the widespread adoption of cryptographic protocols free of weaknesses like this.

Exchange of keys

TLS key exchange describes the process of securely generating an encryption key over an insecure channel. Sometimes described as key agreement or exchange protocols, these protocols use mathematical functions to agree on keys without ever transmitting them in clear text (or in most cases, at all).

There are three main key exchange/agreement protocols in common use with TLS. They are, in approximate order of preference: ECDHE, DHE, and RSA.

ECDHE is based on a Diffie-Hellman exchange, using elliptic curves to agree on a key. Elliptic curve cryptography is very strong, efficient and based on a mathematical problem that remains difficult to solve. It is the ideal choice for security and performance considerations.

DHE is also based on a Diffie-Hellman exchange, except that it uses modular arithmetic to agree on a key, rather than elliptic curves. For these exchanges to be strong, they require keys larger than ECDHE. This is because the mathematics involved for regular DHE is well solved, and we are becoming increasingly adept at solving these problems. So while DHE can provide security similar to ECDHE, it is less efficient at doing so.

RSA key exchange is based on the same asymmetric operations that prove identity for digital signatures (e.g., X.509 certificates). It uses the server's public key to encrypt the shared secret for transmission. This key exchange protocol is widely supported, although it has two main limitations: it requires the use of RSA-based authentication, and it does not provide a perfect transfer secret.

Quantum vulnerability

The security of virtually all public key cryptography currently in use is based on the assumption that factoring large numbers is a difficult, computationally expensive problem. This assumption, however, is invalid when considering quantum computing. Classical computing must rely on a technique known as general numerical field sieving to derive the factors of large numbers. This is a relatively inefficient algorithm. **Shor's algorithm, on the** other hand, is a quantum algorithm that is exponentially more efficient than the general number field sieve. It can be used to quickly break most asymmetric key exchanges, **given a sufficiently powerful quantum computer.**

Quantum-resistant protocols are under development at the time of writing. While nothing is ready for production yet, the looming quantum threat should not prevent the implementation of public key cryptography today. It remains the best tool we have, and cryptographers are working hard to define a clear path. For more information, check out the Post-Quantum Cryptography Conference.

Secret before perfect

PFS, or Perfect Forward Secrecy, is a cryptographic property in which the disclosure of a private key does not result in the compromise of previously negotiated sessions. This is a valuable property because it ensures that an intruder cannot save your session data for later decryption. RSA key exchange does not support PFS because the session key is directly encrypted and transmitted using the private key. DHE or ECDHE must be used to obtain the PFS.

Mind Your Curves

Cryptographic experts have questioned the security of many implementations of key agreements based on elliptic curves. While the mathematical and fundamental principles are sound, a standard set of curves is generally used as input for these functions. These standard curves rely on a set of constants, which must remain secure to maintain the integrity of cryptographic operations performed with the resulting curves.

It is these constants that have been interrogated. Some of the brightest minds in the industry **believe that the constants that are widely available for these purposes have been manipulated by state actors and are compromised**. If this is true, it stands to reason that any elliptic curve encryption implementation that takes advantage of these well-known constants has in fact been secretly subverted.

For this reason, some experts recommend the use of DHE key agreement over ECDHE, despite its better mathematical and performance properties. This is problematic in some places, as not all clients fully support DHE (most famously, Internet Explorer does not support DHE in combination with RSA authentication). In this case, it is recommended to use server-side cipher suites to favor DHE negotiation when available, reverting to ECDHE if necessary.

Authentication

There are three common authentication methods, one of which is being phased out: RSA, DSA and ECDSA.

RSA authentication is overwhelmingly the most common, used in over 99% of web-based TLS resources. In general, RSA is a safe bet as long as a sufficiently large key is used. This caveat raises the concern that we are better at solving the mathematical problem at the heart of the RSA algorithm, requiring key sizes to increase to keep up with progress. Despite this, RSA remains the most popular and most often recommended authentication method.

DSA authentication is no longer recommended. While it is (for the most part) a solid technology, a series of other issues have artificially weakened it, including stubborn adoption and standardization. ECDSA, on the other hand, is the new cousin of DSA and uses elliptical curves to facilitate public/private key pairs.

ECDSA is often touted as the future. It applies all the advantages of elliptic curve cryptography to the authentication component, including a smaller key size and better performance and mathematical properties. However, it is assumed that **ECDSA** authentication is **susceptible to malicious elliptic curves**, as described in "Mind Your Curves".

When deciding between RSA and ECDSA authentication, the breaking of widely published elliptic curves must be carefully considered. The identity trade-off can be catastrophic. In addition, ECDSA is not as widely supported as RSA. With the recognition of these two points, it is fair to say that RSA authentication is still a good choice at the time of writing, despite the existence of a technologically superior algorithm (ECDSA).

Separation of duties

For the purposes of a Zero Trust network, it makes sense to separate the encryption tasks from the application itself (Figure 8-7). The resource we are securing in this case is the device, and as such, it makes sense for this piece to be independent of the workload itself.

It also alleviates a number of pain points, including zero delay mitigation, performance penalties, and auditing. For protocols like IPsec, this separation of duties is part of the design, but this is not the case for TLS. Historically, applications speak TLS directly, loading and configuring shared TLS libraries for remote communication.

We have seen the hard points of this model over and over again. Shared libraries spread across the infrastructure, being consumed by a multitude of projects, all with independent versions and configurations. Some languages have more flexible libraries than others, which limits your ability to apply the latest and greatest. Most importantly, it is very difficult to ensure that all these applications are actually using TLS in the right way and staying up to date with known vulnerabilities.

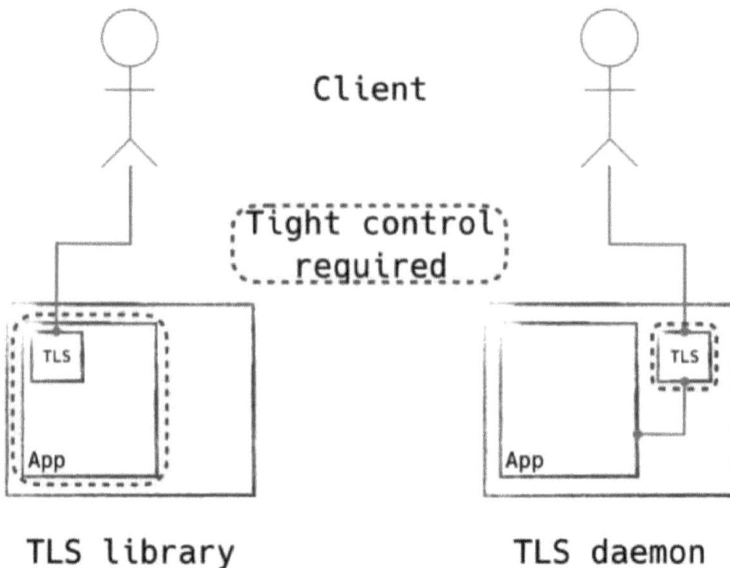

Figure 8-7

To solve the problem, it is useful to move the TLS configuration management to the control plane. Connections to the service are negotiated by the TLS daemon and then passed locally to the application. The TLS daemon is configured with system certificates, trusted authorities, and endpoint information - that's about it.

In this way, we can ensure that all software receives authentication and device security with TLS, regardless of its support. In addition, because whitelisted flows on unapproved networks are zero-rated, we can ensure that application traffic is protected by limiting whitelisted flows to known TLS endpoints.

Bulk encryption

All of the complexities and components of TLS discussed thus far apply primarily to the initial TLS handshake. TLS handshake has two primary purposes: authentication and session key creation.

TLS handshakes are computationally expensive due to the mathematical operations required to validate them. This is a trade-off between security and performance. While we strongly desire this level of security, the performance impact is prohibitive if we apply these operations to all communications.

Asymmetric cryptography is extraordinarily important in the process of secure entry and authentication, but its strength can be matched with symmetric cryptography as long as identity or authentication is not an issue. Symmetric encryption uses a single secret key instead of a public/private key pair, and is less computationally expensive than asymmetric cryptography by an order of magnitude. This is where the concept of a TLS handshake and session keys comes in.

Some very clever mathematicians and cryptographers realized that we could use both strong and expensive operations to securely generate a unique secret - one that can be shared between parties (Figure 8-8). The key exchange component of TLS is the one that generates this shared key and ensures that both parties know about it.

This shared key is then used as input to a symmetric encryption algorithm, which is applied to all session traffic after contact is made. This methodology ensures that the entire session benefits from the strength of asymmetric cryptography without inheriting the performance implications associated with asymmetric encryption schemes.

When it comes to choices for bulk encryption algorithms, TLS supports several, but the recommendation is pretty well aligned across the board: just use AES. It checks all the desirable boxes, including the fact that it's unpatented, widely implemented in hardware, and practically

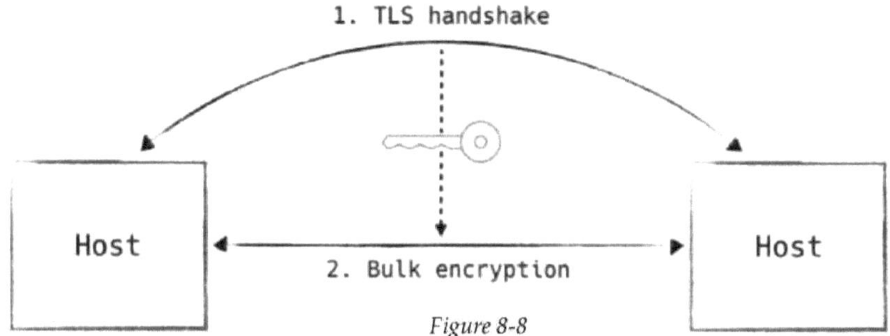

Figure 8-8

universally implemented in software. It performs very well, is highly controlled / scrutinized, and remains uninterrupted to the best of public knowledge. Many people say that "AES is pretty good", and while that can be a hard pill to swallow when it comes to security protocols, such a statement has never been closer to the truth.

Message authentication

When communicating securely, message authenticity is an important, if not mandatory, property. Encryption ensures confidentiality, but without message authenticity, how do you ensure the integrity of that message? Without an error in decryption, it is difficult or impossible to distinguish a forged message from a genuine one.

Some encryption modes (such as AES-GCM) provide guarantees of message confidentiality and authenticity simultaneously. However, these guarantees are only applicable during bulk encryption; there are several TLS exchanges that are not protected by the bulk transfer specification, and the message authenticity scheme protects them as well.

Explicit authenticity sometimes required

Since some bulk encryption algorithms provide message integrity guarantees, it is not always necessary to perform explicit authenticity checks on every packet. Instead, TLS will prefer built-in guarantees for bulk transfers and will rely on explicit authenticity checks for all packets not associated with the bulk transfer (e.g., TLS control messages).

As far as choice goes, the options are limited to MD5 and the SHA family of hashes. The former has been cryptographically broken for some time now, leaving the SHA family as the only reasonable choice for ensuring message integrity under TLS. There are even concerns when using the weaker SHA variant, SHA-1, as it is now considered vulnerable to ever-increasing computing power. As such, it is recommended to choose the strongest SHA hash that can be reasonably deployed, given the hardware and software constraints.

In addition, it is recommended that block ciphers with built-in authentication be used whenever possible, as they are generally more efficient and secure than relying on a disjoint authentication mechanism. TLS version 1.3 requires the use of authenticated encryption.

Mutually authenticated TLS for device authentication

Just like any other protocol used for device authentication, TLS comes with its ups and downs.

The first is that, because of its position in the network stack, TLS is protocol dependent.

It is most often implemented as a TCP-based protocol, although a UDP-based variant called DTLS is also available. The presence of DTLS highlights the deficiency of TLS' position in the stack. With this, TLS suffers diminishing returns when used to secure IP protocols other than those it natively supports, such as TCP or UDP.

Another thing to consider is the automation requirement. TLS is typically deployed as an infrastructure service in perimeter networks by leveraging intermediaries that are typically positioned at the perimeter. However, this mode of operation is unsuitable for a zero-trust network as long as the intermediary and the upstream endpoint are separated by a computer network. In a zero-trust network, applications running a TLS-speaking intermediary must be on the same host as the intermediary itself. Therefore, protecting data center zero-trust networks with TLS requires additional automation to configure applications to speak through this external security layer. It does not come "free" like other protocols such as IPsec.

All that said, it remains the best choice today for protecting zero-trust networks from clients. TLS is widely supported in both software and transit (i.e., intermediate networks worldwide), and can be used for simple and reliable operation. Most web browsers natively support the mutually authenticated TLS protocol, which means that resources can be protected using zero-trust principles without the immediate need for specialized client-side software.

Filtering

Filtering is the process by which packets are admitted or rejected by systems on a network. When most people think of filtering, they usually think of a firewall, a service or device that sits between the network and the application to filter traffic entering or leaving that device. Firewalls provide filtering, but they can provide other services, such as network address translation (NAT), traffic shaping and VPN tunneling services. Filtering can be provided by other systems that are not traditionally considered, such as routers or managed switches. It is important to remember that filtering is a simple service that can be applied at multiple locations in a networked system.

Filtering can be quite frustrating for non-security-minded users, as it blocks the desired network communication. Wouldn't it be better to get rid of this nuisance and assume that the user knows what they want? Unfortunately, well-meaning users may trivially expose services that they would prefer not to expose upon further inspection. In the early days of permanent Internet connections, users' computers were routinely exposed to file sharing and Internet chat services. Filtering provides a type of check and balance for network communication, forcing users to consider whether a particular connection should cross a sensitive boundary.

Many of the zero-trust concepts to date have focused on advanced encryption and authentication systems. Indeed, these aspects of network security are not as prevalent in network designs as they should be. However, we should not minimize the importance of network filtering. It is still a critical component of a zero-trust architecture, and so we will explore it in three parts: - Host filtering

Traffic filtering on
Host - Reserved filtering

Filtering traffic through a peer host in the network - Intermediate filtering

Filtering traffic through devices between two hosts

Host filtering

Host filtering replaces a network endpoint to actively participate in its own security. The goal is to ensure that each host is configured to filter its own network traffic. This is different from traditional network design, where filtering is delegated to a centralized system away from the host.

Centralized filtering is most often implemented using a hardware firewall. These firewalls use application-specific integrated circuits (ASICs) to efficiently process packets flowing through the device. Since the device is often a shared resource for many core systems, these ASICs are essential to perform the task of filtering the overall traffic of all these systems. The use of ASICs provides raw performance at the expense of flexibility.

Software firewalls, like those found in modern operating systems, are much more flexible than their hardware counterparts. They offer a full set of services, such as setting policies based on time and an arbitrary offset value. Many of these software firewalls can be extended with new modules to provide additional services.

Unlike the early days of the Internet, all modern desktop and server operating systems now offer some form of network filtering via a host-based firewall: - Linux

iptables -
BSD systems

Berkley Packet Filter (BPF)
- macOS

Additional application firewall and host firewall available via command line - Windows

Windows Firewall service

Perhaps surprisingly, neither iOS nor Android comes with a host-based firewall. Apple's IOS Security Guide notes that it considers a firewall unnecessary since the attack surface is reduced on iOS "by limiting listening ports and removing unnecessary network utilities such as telnet, shells, or a web server." Google does not publish an official security guide. Android, perhaps because of its ability to run non-Play Store approved software, has third-party firewalls to install if a user chooses to do so.

Zero Trust systems assume that the network is hostile. As a result, they filter network traffic at all possible points, often using host-based firewalls. Adding a host-based firewall reduces the attack surface of a host by filtering out unwanted network traffic. Although software firewalls do not have the same throughput capabilities as hardware systems, the fact that the filtering is distributed across the system (and thus on a portion of the overall traffic) often results in little performance degradation.

Using host-based filtering is easy to use. Configuration management systems support host-based firewalling very well. When writing logic to install services, it is easier to capture allowed connections right next to one's installation and configuration routines. Conversely, filtering in a remote system is more difficult because exceptions are separated from the application that needs them.

Host-based firewalls also provide opportunities for new uses of programmable filtering. Single packet authorization (SPA), discussed earlier in this chapter, is an excellent example of this idea. SPA programmatically manages the host-based firewall to reduce the attack surface of a service on a host. This is advantageous because, on occasion, carefully crafted malicious packets can be built to exploit a weakness in network services. For example, a service may require authentication and authorization before processing a request, but the authentication logic may contain a buffer overflow error that an attacker can use to implement a remote code execution vulnerability. By introducing a filtering layer, we can hide the more complex service interface behind a simpler system that handles firewall rules.

There are of course problems with using host-based firewalls exclusively for network filtering. One such problem is the possibility that a co-located firewall could become meaningless if a host were to be compromised. An attacker who is able to access a host and elevate its privilege can remove the host firewall or adjust its configuration. Needless to say, this is a big problem, as it removes a layer of defense in the system. This concern is why filtering has traditionally been handled by a separate device, away from potentially dangerous hosts.

This approach highlights the benefits of isolation in security design, which could benefit host-based filtering. As the industry moves towards isolation techniques such as virtualization and containerization, it becomes clear that these technologies offer the opportunity to further isolate host-based filtering. Without these technologies, the only form of isolation available is local user privilege. On a Unix-based system, for example, only the root user is able to make changes to the firewall configuration. In a virtualized system, however, one could implement filtering outside the virtual machine, which provides strong safeguards against attacks on the filtering system. In fact, this is how Amazon's security group feature is implemented, as shown in Figure 8-9.

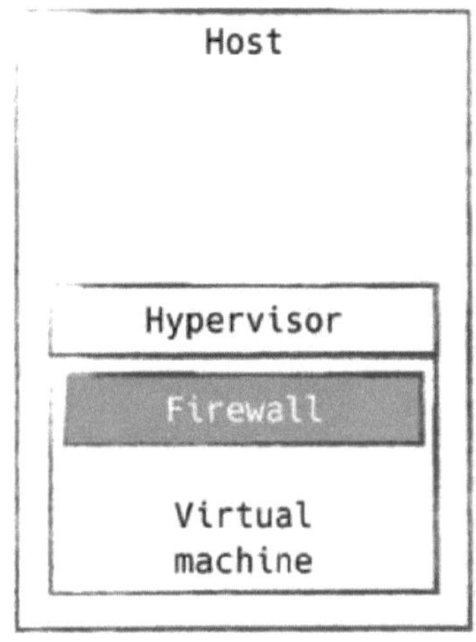

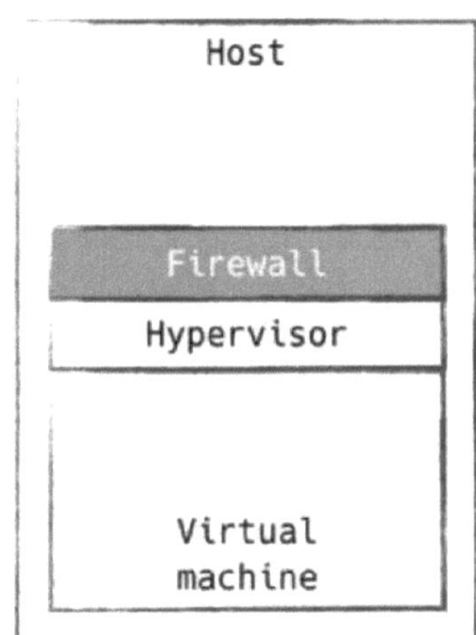

Figure 8-9

Another problem with host-based filtering is the cost associated with deep network filtering. Imagine a scenario where a large percentage of traffic is filtered by host-based filtering. By applying filtering closest to the destination system, the network incurs an additional cost to forward these packets, only for them to be ultimately discarded. This situation also raises the possibility of a denial-of-service attack forcing the network infrastructure to carry large volumes of unnecessary traffic, as well as overwhelming the relatively weaker software firewalls. For this reason, while host-based firewalls are the best place to start thinking about filtering, they present a risk if they are the only place where filtering occurs. We will discuss ways to push filtering into the network in "Intermediary Filtering".

Screening with reservation

Bookended filtering is the act of applying policy not only on receiving a packet, but also on sending them. This mode of filtering is not common in traditional networks. It brings some interesting advantages to network design, which we will now explore.

Egress (the opposite of ingress) is a term used to describe network traffic that leaves a host. This type of filtering is commonly used to manage communication from a private network to public networks, but it is rarely used in a private network. There are a few reasons why this is the case: - Ingress filtering is easier to reason about, as listening services can be enumerated when creating firewall rules. Output filtering requires more accounting to capture how hosts intend to communicate.

- Ingress filtering is generally considered good enough to stop unwanted communication in the network.
- Output filtering requires knowledge of all expected flows, which is generally not the case in traditional networks.

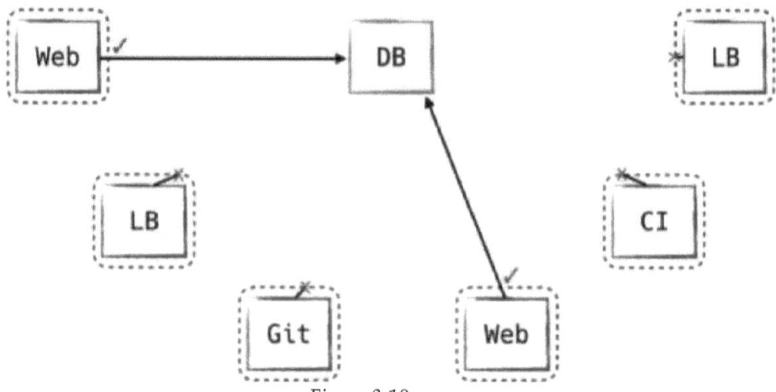

Figure 8-10

Bookended filtering uses the output filtering in the Zero Trust network to harden the system. We can see how this hardening is beneficial with the example in Figure 8-10. Consider a system in which a database server has input filtering rules configured to allow access from application servers. A well-meaning administrator investigates some network connectivity issues. In the process of their investigation, the administrator relaxes the database input filtering to rule out the possibility that the problem was caused. Basically, this administrator forgets to roll back their change after disproving this theory. This error removes a layer of defense in the system for a period of time. Even worse, discovering this lost defense can be difficult because the expected communication (from the application servers to the database server) continues to work.

In this scenario, a network that has ubiquitous bookended filtering is protected even when this critical configuration is in the system. In some ways, this is similar to herd immunity - the collective benefit a community provides to unvaccinated members when the vast majority of members are vaccinated against a disease. Instead of preventing disease, bookended filtering protects misconfigured systems from the potential impact of that misconfiguration.

Building bookended filtering into a system is not as hard as it sounds, given the right conditions. Communication flows must be captured in a way that can be programmatically consumed. The best way to capture these flows is to define fine-grained input rules. These input rules should allow access to a service based on each client's server role instead of broadly opening access to a service. By capturing this detail, we have built a dependency graph from which output rules can be computed and applied throughout the system.

As we saw in host filtering, egress filtering is best applied when isolated from the applications running in the system. The same ideas apply here: prefer to implement filtering on the other side of a virtualized or containerized environment to have the most robust filtering mechanisms. Beyond the implementation of filtering, it is important to consider the isolation of the data used to build the output filtering rules. It may seem attractive to compute this data from a dynamic data source such as a service discovery system, but bookended filtering is most effective when the stream database is isolated from the running system. Instead, use a database that changes slowly, especially one that requires a human to review the changes.

CALICO Project

Project Calico is a virtual network system for dynamically scheduled workloads. A workload is a generic term that applies to any application that needs to run in a data center.

This application can be inside a container or a virtual machine. Calico takes the lessons learned in operating the Internet and brings them into the data center to create a simpler network that can scale efficiently as its network size increases.

Calico is not a total zero-trust solution, but it does echo some of the ideas of zero-trust networks. Calico distributes filtering throughout the network, which is applied to host machines. These hosts are dynamically reconfigured based on changes in a database that describes the entire network. This design is very similar to the host filtering we discussed earlier.

Calico also includes the bookended filtering concepts we discussed. This means that hosts at both ends of a connection filter traffic based on their knowledge of which connections to allow. This dual enforcement of network communication is considered a secondary defense in the network.

Intermediate filtering

Intermediate filtering is the idea that devices other than the sender or receiver can and should participate in filtering traffic in a zero-trust network. This means at a minimum, perimeter filtering can play a role in a zero-trust network, and at a maximum, intermediate devices in the network.

As we saw in "Host Filtering", filtering traffic only at the destination incurs an additional cost on the network when the rate of unwanted traffic is very high. High rate filtered traffic will most often come from incoming traffic to the Internet. Ideally, we want to filter traffic as soon as possible to reduce the impact and cost of filtering. For this application, filtering on perimeter systems located between the Zero Trust network and the Internet is ideal. These devices typically need to be hardware-based to effectively filter packets entering the system.

Perimeter filters can also be an important check and balance in a zero trust network. Perimeter filters should be a combination of global rules and coarse-grained host rules. By keeping the global rules separate from the host policy, invariants regarding the external network configuration are defined.

Exceptions to this rule must be traceable to the host infrastructure that relies on these exceptions and the actions taken to instantiate them. The best implementation derives these exceptions from the host policies themselves. By tying the host policy to the exception policy, the system will be more consistent as hosts come and go on the network. However, these exceptions must be checked to be as tight as possible. A review process should be put in place for all policy changes to guard against overly broad exceptions that could compromise the security of the system.

UPnP considered harmful

Deriving perimeter policies from host policies should not be confused with UPnP, a technology used to reconfigure consumer firewalls. UPnP is rightly criticized because any application on the network can reconfigure the perimeter. In the zero-approval model, there is a chain of trust between host policies and exceptions created on the perimeter.

It may seem strange that we are discussing perimeter filtering in such a positive way, given the failings of the perimeter model. The key detail to understand here is that zero-trust networks do not reject all perimeter concepts. Instead, they encourage administrators to start at the host and work their way out. Perimeter devices ultimately play a role in this, with denial-of-service mitigation being by far the most notable application.

An interesting idea in zero-trust networks is to use the host policy database to dynamically schedule the network structure itself. This would result in a software defined network (SDN) that does not blindly route packets to the destination, but actively manages the switching and routing policy based on expected and allowed flows. This leads to a few advantages: - Potentially malicious traffic is kept away from the hosts, reducing the attack surface.

- Software firewalls on hosts are augmented by the network itself, adding additional layers of defense into the network.

Like the perimeter filtering described above, in-network filtering should be considered an enhancement to the base layer of host-based filtering. It should not replace it.

Transfer and routing authorization

As we discuss filtering, a theme emerges: zero-trust networks take advantage of relatively slow network details to distribute the application, resulting in a more secure network. This observation opens up an interesting opportunity: can we propagate the application across the network infrastructure, effectively elevating these channels from a simple packet transmission system to an intelligent network?

Imagine an SDN controller that has only installed flow instructions based on the result of a strong authentication and authorization process. A client wishing to access a network resource can signal the control plane, providing the network access request with appropriate credentials. Upon successful authorization of the request, the network is installed and available, but only for the specific authorized flow.

Summary

This chapter has focused on how traffic gains trust in an untrusted network. We have noted the distinctions between encryption and authenticity - two related but distinct concepts. Zero trust networks require authenticity in communication, and most networks also have an interest in having their traffic encrypted.

We have explored the first packet problem in network communications. Modern authentication systems are quite complex systems, which results in a large attack surface. We talked about hiding these services behind a single packet authorization system, which is a relatively simple service that can be used to hide a more complex authentication system like TLS.

We then discussed two competing protocols for encryption and authentication of network traffic: TLS and IPsec. We discussed the difference between these systems and made it clear that mutually authenticated TLS is best suited for client/server interactions or in heterogeneous environments, while IPsec seems well suited for the data center (especially when network address translation is absent).

Zero Trust networks always need packet filtering capabilities that they deploy throughout the network. We have described three types of filtering that can be deployed in such a network: host, bookended, and intermediate filtering. Each type of filtering adds robustness to the network and can be deployed in the network using system automation and a shared database of expected network communication.

The next chapter takes all the concepts we've learned so far and presents a plan for creating your own Zero Trust Network.

Chapter 9: Building a Zero Trust network

This chapter will help readers develop a strategy for taking the knowledge in the previous chapters and applying it to their system. Zero Trust networks are very likely to be built around existing systems, so this chapter will focus on how to make that transition successfully.

It is important to remember that zero trust is not a product that can be locked into the network. It is a set of architectural principles that are applied according to the needs and constraints of the network. Therefore, this chapter cannot provide a checklist of changes to be made, but rather a framework for how to approach achieving zero trust in a network in your own system.

Choose the scope

Before you start building a zero trust network, it is important to choose the right scope for the effort. A very mature Zero Trust network will have many interactive systems. For a large organization, building these systems may be feasible, but for small organizations, the number and complexity of these systems may make a zero trust network out of reach.

It's important to remember that the zero-trust architecture is an ideal to work with rather than a list of requirements that must be met completely from day one. This is no different from perimeter-based networks. Less mature networks may initially choose a simple network design to reduce administration complexity. As the network evolves and the risk of breach increases, the network will need to be redesigned to better isolate systems.

Although the zero-trust network design is an ideal, not all design features are equally valuable. Determining which components are required and which are nice will have a big impact on the success of a zero trust implementation.

What is really required?

Limiting the scope of a Zero Trust network necessarily requires prioritizing the set of properties presented earlier in this book. This RFC-style prioritization list is the author's opinion of how this work should be prioritized:
- All network flows MUST be authenticated before being processed.
- All network streams SHOULD be encrypted before being transmitted.

- Authentication and encryption MUST be performed by the endpoints in the network.
- All network flows MUST be enumerated in order for access to be applied by the system.
- The most powerful authentication and encryption suites SHOULD be used in the network.
- Authentication SHOULD NOT rely on public PKI providers. Private PKI systems should be used instead.
- The devices SHOULD be regularly scanned, patched and rotated.

<u>**RFC-style priority lists**</u>

RFC documents are the lingua franca for proposed changes to the Internet infrastructure. In these documents, the language and structure are clearly defined to allow readers to more quickly understand the changes proposed in this document.

One aspect of this language that is very useful in the prioritization discussion is the standard terms defined in RFC 2119. This RFC defines a set of terms (MUST / MUST NOT, SHOULD / SHOULD NOT, MAY / MAY NOT) that carry more weight than their normal usage in the common literature.

The priority list in this book uses these terms with similar intent to their definitions in RFC 2119. Although architectural features do not have the same requirements as protocol designs, the use of these standard terms is intended to echo the usage presented in this RFC.

For completeness, here are the intended definitions of these standard terms when used in this book:
MUST
This term is used for a requirement for the implemented system to be considered compatible with the zero confidence design.
-   MUST NOT
This is the opposite of MUST. A system intending to implement the zero-trust design is required not to have this feature.
-   SHOULD
This term refers to an architectural feature that is desired in a zero-trust network, but given that cost constraints can be described. When prioritizing this feature, system administrators must be aware that they are trading off the security of their systems for lower cost to implement them. Wherever possible, system administrators should avoid compromising on these features as the benefit of not compromising them is seen as justifying the initial cost of implementing them.
-   SHOULD NOT
It is the opposite of SHOULD.
CAN

This term is used for architectural features of a network of zero trust that provide value, but are considered nice to have. System administrators should plan to implement these aspects once they have built a system that meets the MUST and SHOULD definitions. It is important to note that these additional features add value to the network by hardening it, so they should not be considered a net loss.

With this prioritized list of design requirements for building a zero-trust network, let's explain why particular requirements were categorized as they were.

All network flows MUST be authenticated before being processed
In a zero-trust network, all packets received by the system are immediately suspect. As such, they must be rigorously inspected before the data they contain can be processed. Strong authentication is the primary mechanism by which we accomplish this.

Authentication is absolutely necessary in order to gain confidence in the provenance of network data. It is perhaps the most important element of a network without trust. Without it, we have nothing and are forced to place our trust in the network.

All network streams SHOULD be encrypted before being transmitted

A key lesson of this book is that a network link cannot be trusted to reliably transmit data or signals from one system to another. The physical accessibility of a network link to dangerous actors makes it trivial to compromise. Moreover, even in a physically secure network, bad actors can digitally infiltrate a system and passively probe the network for valuable data.

By encrypting data on a device before transmitting it over the network, we reduce the attack surface of that communication to the reliability of the device itself, namely the security of the application and the physical device.

Authentication and encryption MUST be performed by application layer endpoints

Because Zero-Trust networks recognize the threat that trusted network links pose to a system's security, it is important that secure communications are established between application layer endpoints. Adding middleware components that support these responsibilities (such as VPN concentrators or TLS-terminated load balancers) can leave upstream network communications exposed to physical and virtual threats.

Therefore, a system that claims to be a zero clearance is required to implement encryption and authentication at every application layer endpoint on the network.

All network flows MUST be enumerated so that access can be applied by the system

Zero Trust networks depend on the data that defines the expected network characteristics. Therefore, defining all expected network flows is critical to safeguarding the network.

We should be careful to note that enumerating flows does not require onerous change management controls to provide value. A simple process of defining expected flows provides tremendous value in terms of network enforcement and change auditing.

Without the list of expected network flows, zero-approval systems cannot highlight unexpected communications that need attention from administrators or should be denied.

The author strongly believes that deferring the effort of enumerating flows will ultimately result in a task list that is deemed unachievable. The author believes that the best way to maintain this database of expected flows is to distribute the responsibility for defining these flows throughout the organization. When distributing this responsibility, organizations must take precautions to educate teams on best practices for change management to guard against insider threats to the system. One such threat is allowing a single person to update the flow database without any oversight. A simple review system can mitigate this threat.

Flow data as a source of truth

Creating a database of expected flows is best accomplished by making the flow database the data source for authorizing this access. By configuring this dependency (and disallowing external modifications), the stream database will be consistent with the actual authorized access.

When capturing flows, following these rules will improve data quality: - Capture the intended use of a flow with the details of the strategy (for example,

LB access - from LB hosts to the web application).
- Prefer narrowly defined flows over wide access.

The most powerful authentication and encryption suites available SHOULD be used in the network

Zero Trust networks assume a hostile network environment. Strong authentication and encryption suites are therefore an important component of Zero Trust network security.

Suites that offer strong security unfortunately change, so this book cannot offer specific choices that will stand the test of time. Readers should refer to security standards such as the NIST encryption guidelines to choose robust encryption suites.

System administrators should always aim for the most powerful suites possible, but device and application functionality can limit the types of suites available. In these cases, administrators should be aware that by reducing the power of these suites, security is compromised in their network.

Authentication SHOULD NOT rely on public PKI providers - private PKI systems should be used instead

Public PKI systems provide trust assurances to unmanaged endpoints in a secure communication. A certificate authority signs certificates used to establish secure communications. The endpoint receiving this signed certificate is able to verify its authenticity by comparing the signing material to the list of trusted certificate authorities already present on the system. By associating systems with a list of trusted public certificate authorities, endpoints can establish secure communication channels with systems they have not previously communicated with.

Given the advantages that public PKI offers for building secure communication channels, why do zero-trust networks prefer private PKI systems? The reason, perhaps unsurprisingly given zero-trust's emphasis on trust management, is that third-party trust places the system at increased risk. There are several risks that the public PKI system brings to a zero trust network.

One concern is the number of public certification authorities that are considered trustworthy. With the increase in Internet traffic, the number of trusted public certificate authorities has grown. Any of these trusted certificate authorities has the potential to sign a fraudulent certificate that incorrectly asserts the trustworthiness of a malicious system. Certificate pinning can contribute to this risk by giving an endpoint knowledge of which certificate to expect for a given endpoint, but certificate pinning requires the endpoint to have prior knowledge of the expected certificate, which poses a new challenge.

The use of a public certificate authority also presents another threat. State actors have become more aggressive in using judicial powers to compel organizations to act against the trust assurances they provide to their customers. These demands increasingly use laws that prohibit the parties involved from disclosing their actions. Given this aggressive stance, allowing state actors into the trust mechanisms of a zero-trust network should give system administrators pause.

Based on these concerns, zero-trust networks should prefer private PKI systems. Endpoints should be configured to allow only certificates signed by the private PKI system. We discussed PKI in more detail in Chapter 2.

The devices SHOULD be regularly scanned, corrected and rotated

We learned in Chapter 5 that device security is critical to building a zero-trust network. Administrators must build in the assumption that trusted devices on the network are compromised and, therefore, build defenses into device management to mitigate this threat.

To this end, devices should be scanned on a regular basis to capture the software running or installed on the device at any given time. Scanning can be used to discover and prevent known malware from running on the device, but administrators should operate under the assumption that malware prevention software (e.g., antivirus software) will always be imperfect. Rather than focusing all of their energy on stopping malware execution, administrators should focus on creating forensic capabilities so that they can analyze the impact of an inevitable malware attack.

Keeping devices fresh is also very important. System administrators should have a plan to regularly install the latest security patches. Also, a regular device rotation policy ensures that devices do not accumulate, which can compromise the security of that system.

Prefer re-imaging over long-term analysis and remediation

Device reliability degrades over time due to the increased risk of a device being compromised. Reacting regularly to devices, while disrupting, ensures that confidence in the fleet remains high. Aim to reimage servers once a quarter and personal devices every two years.

Build a system diagram

Constructing a system diagram is an important first step towards achieving a zero-trust network. Having a clear picture of how internal and external network communication occurs will be useful when designing the system's communication channels.

System diagrams, such as the one shown in Figure 9-1, are often maligned for being horribly out of date. These diagrams are usually constructed by hand, which requires a great deal of human effort. Given the speed at which diagrams become outdated, there is a widespread view that system diagrams are simply not worth the investment. This view, however, misses the benefit of having a human-centric view of how the system should be built. While an engineer can read code or interrogate existing systems to determine how the system is built, this does not provide any insight into whether this state was desired or accidental.

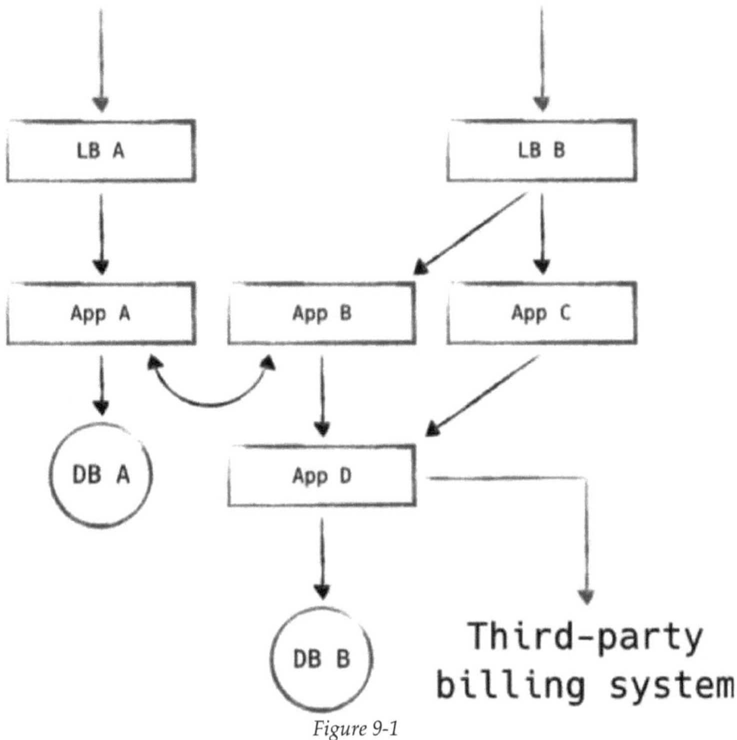

Figure 9-1

So, while system diagrams are useful, but often outdated, the natural question is how much time and effort should we spend creating them. A good path to an existing network is to first observe the communication that flows through the network. You can capture this communication using tools that record flows. Once the flow information is captured, creating a system diagram will be an exercise in categorizing the communication classes.

In the next section, we will discuss tools for capturing and categorizing network flows, as well as a strategy for breaking down this large effort into smaller chunks of work.

Understanding your flows

A network flow is a temporal communication between a source system and a destination. A single flow can be mapped directly to an entire conversation when using a bidirectional transport protocol (e.g., TCP). For unidirectional transport protocols (e.g., UDP), a single flow can only capture half of a network conversation. Indeed, while two UDP flows may be logically related, an observer on the network may be unable to make this association without a deep understanding of the application data.

Capturing all flow activity in an existing production network is a logical first step for a system that wants to move to a zero trust model. Logging flows in a network over a long period of time is a non-invasive way to discover which network connections exist and need to be accounted for in the new security model. Without this initial information gathering, efforts to move to a zero-trust model will result in frequent network communication problems, making the project too intrusive and disruptive.

<u>**Ways to discover the flows**</u>

There are many different mechanisms for logging and analyzing network flows. The system used will depend largely on the type of network being run (physical or virtual) and the level of access an administrator has to endpoints.

Physical networks have rich access capabilities to the raw packets that flow through the network. Business-Class switches will typically have the ability to mirror packets to a second port on the switch (known as a SPAN or mirror port). This approach is relatively safe to enable on a lightly loaded switch, but it does mask certain types of errors in the network. TAP devices, which are placed in-line in the network link, ensure that all data is transmitted to a monitoring device. For the purpose of discovering logical flows in the network, either approach will work.

Virtualized networks may have the ability to inspect network traffic, but they typically operate at a coarser level. Amazon Web Services, for example, has a feature that records every flow in a network, which can be used to analyze traffic on its systems.

Discovering flows through the network gives perfect visibility into the traffic flowing through, but it is difficult to link this analysis to individual applications without an endpoint monitoring system. In cases where endpoint monitoring is feasible, network flow discovery on the endpoints themselves can provide a more detailed view of the source of traffic in the system. Software firewalls running in log-only mode can be a useful tool for discovering flows in the system without impacting communication.

On Linux endpoints, there are several approaches to discovering and cataloging network flows, which Harald Welte's article "Flow-based network accounting with Linux" captures.

With all network flows recorded, the next goal is to categorize the flows according to the top-level system connections. These connections should be defined at the logical system level instead of the individual IP/port level. The connections defined with this exercise are very valuable data. With the definitions in hand, one is able to better enforce known connections and become aware of changes in communication patterns within a network. Since many secure network operations can be derived from this database of connections, it is clear that capturing this mapping is very useful.

For a very large network, capturing and categorizing all network flows could be a huge undertaking. The natural question is whether capturing all network connections is required for the transition to a zero-trust network. Fortunately, a zero-trust network can be achieved incrementally within an existing perimeter-based system. Existing perimeter or network boundaries can be leveraged to build a zero-trust network on either side of the boundary. The zero-trust model can then propagate from zone to zone as in Figure 9-3, improving the network security of the existing system while maintaining the operational security measures already in place.

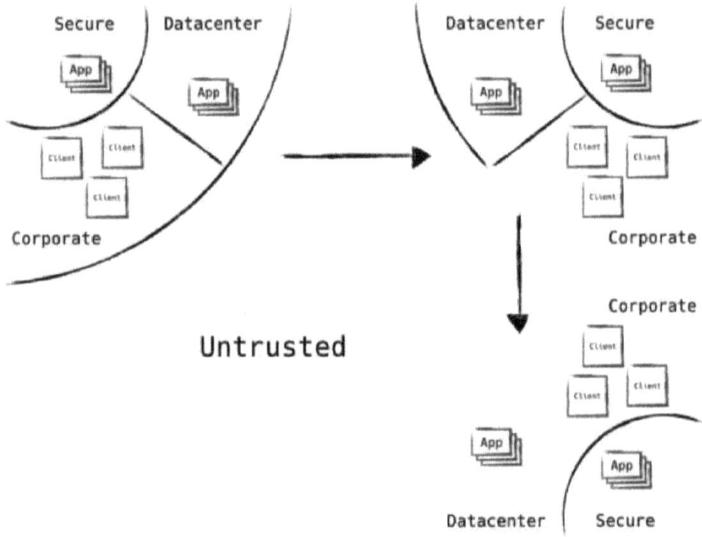

Figure 9-3

Controllerless architecture

A fully mature Zero Trust network will have at its core several control plane systems that provide critical security services. While having these systems is ideal, it is possible to iterate towards the idealized deployment while using common infrastructure systems initially. We will explore some of these systems now.

"Cheating with configuration management

Many operationally mature organizations use configuration management tools to manage their infrastructure. When using these systems, the desired configuration state is captured and controlled by the version. After examining the current state of the system, the configuration management system uses this desired configuration to calculate the changes that will bring the system to the desired state. Using a configuration management tool provides a number of advantages over planned changes performed by humans
the fleet.
- Configuration data can be stored in a version control system, which provides a useful record of what changes were made and why.
- Configuration drift is less likely to occur because its status is monitored by the configuration management system.

The first way that configuration management is often deployed is to manage the configuration of individual computers. Systems are booted from a known blank list (usually just the initial installation of the operating system), and then reconfigured into the desired state based on that machine's role in the infrastructure. Automating this process makes it easier to replace the infrastructure.

While there is much value in using configuration management for this task, these tools can also be used as a general automation framework. For example, they can be used to configure encryption primitives between infrastructure hosts or to punch tightly bounded holes in host-based firewalls. In this way, configuration management (or CM) systems can be used to drive a subset of the functions normally offered by a mature zero-trust control plane.

Similarly, CM systems can also be used to build useful abstractions in the network. Most CM tools support mechanisms to extend the set of available resources or actions. Using this extension point, it is possible to build more complex resources into the system. For example, one could define the concept of a service resource that would capture all the standard infrastructure that should be used to make the service available on the network.

CM is a temporary springboard

Configuration management systems are best deployed so that the system achieves a stable configuration. With this ideal in mind, using a configuration management system to make frequent changes to the system seems counterproductive. We should not dismiss this concern, as it has some validity. Instead, we should be aware that using a configuration management system to build a zero-trust network is just a stepping stone to the ideal solution, which would shift these responsibilities to a dedicated controller.

Authentication and application authorization

A typical organization uses many services, with client-side delivery increasingly browser-based. Since a zero-approval network does not infer approval based on the network address of a connection, each service must manage authentication and authorization.

A simple solution is to store the username and passwords in each application. This approach, however, is strongly discouraged, mainly because of the complexity of management.

Instead of having each application implement its own authentication systems, applications should integrate with an identity provider system that can provide centralized authentication and authorization checks. SAML (Security Assertion Markup Language) is a technology that can be used to integrate an application with an identity provider. OAuth2 is another.

This is not to say that an application should have no authorization responsibilities. On the contrary, it is expected that some application-level permissions exist, especially when considering things like varying user permissions. The overhead of account management, user authentication, and high-level authorization/access can be offloaded while leaving room for application-centric authorization.

When authenticating with an identity provider, multi-factor authentication must be used to ensure that the user's credentials cannot be easily stolen. We discussed multifactor authentication in Chapter 6.

Authentication of load balancers and proxies

Many service architectures require the use of a load balancer to distribute requests to a set of primary hosts. Often, these load balancers represent the boundary between a client-oriented system and a data center system. This can create confusion about how to properly apply zero-trust controls in such a system, as the client-facing semantics of zero-trust can be quite different from those of server-side systems.

In Chapter 7, we discussed application authentication and authorization management as an analog to user authentication and authorization. In back-end systems, the best way to authorize an application is to inject ephemeral credentials at runtime, whether it's an API key, a short-lived certificate, or something else. Each piece of credentials represents only one instance of a running application.

In a load-balanced system, the load-balancing software itself can be viewed as a server-side application. Each instance of the software is started with ephemeral credentials that identify the instance to upstream hosts. This is in addition to device authentication, which occurs between the load balancer and the upstream system using the techniques presented in Chapter 5.

With this architecture, the load balancer can manage the authentication and authorization responsibilities of users and clients, relying on identity providers as needed. Information from the authentication and authorization process (such as username) can then be sent with the original request to the primary hosts. In this way, the zero-trust architecture can be preserved as data crosses client-server boundaries and enters the data center.

Prefer security tokens over TOTP

When multifactor authentication was first deployed in organizations, users had simple devices that continuously generated time-based tokens. With the prevalence of smartphones today, most users prefer to use a multifactor app on their smartphone to generate codes.

Protocols that use security tokens, such as U2F, are increasingly preferred over time-based token systems because of their protection against phishing attacks. It's a bonus that these systems are also generally easier for users to use. If possible, prefer security tokens over TOTP systems. We discussed these technologies in Chapter 6.

Relationship-based policy

Zero trust advocates a control plane that injects the results of authorization decisions into the network to enable secure communication. In this model, each network flow is individually authenticated and authorized. Enforcement is achieved by reconfiguring or signaling the network structure to enable authorized communication.

In a small-scale zero-trust network, which lacks these control plan systems, we are forced to reduce this ambition. Instead of

To build a network that uses dynamic injection and signaling, we can build a system that defines policies at the relationship level.

In a relationship-oriented network policy, communication between two devices is defined and controlled via traditional network filtering mechanisms such as firewalls and required TLS connections. These policy enforcement mechanisms may seem very similar to a perimeter-based model. The main difference in the relationship-oriented model is that the policy is tightly bound to the communicating devices instead of communicating network segments. This approach is sometimes called microperimeterization.

By capturing and enforcing which devices should communicate with each other, we build a database of expected communication that will be of great value in the future when dynamic policy systems decide whether to allow a network flow.

Policy distribution

A common feature of a scaled-down version of zero trust is the distribution of policy (as opposed to just enforcement) throughout the network. Given the detailed policy decisions we expect in the network, automation is essential to make the network operational.

In a mature Zero-Trust network, policy interpretation is handled entirely by control plane systems, which can dynamically reconfigure the infrastructure and network devices, or give authorization responses to signaling enforcement components.

In a controllerless deployment, however, we need to use a different mechanism. Configuration management systems can be used to fill this gap in the network control plane.

Devices can be dynamically configured to implement their own enforcement of expected network communication. Configuring a host-based software firewall that is computed from the relationship rules database can provide a less difficult per-host enforcement than a centralized physical firewall. Communications can also be authorized by hosts via mechanisms such as mutually authenticated TLS, again controlled by configuration management software.

The key realization here is that by using existing configuration management systems, we are able to build a virtual control plane that can distribute application responsibilities across the network. While this approach is pragmatic, it is not without its drawbacks: - Forcing hosts to enforce the policy may result in the removal or

change this policy if the host is compromised. In compatible environments, transferring this responsibility across an isolation boundary (e.g., a hypervisor, the host operating system in containerized systems, or network security groups) provides better protection.

- Changes via configuration management systems often have a longer period of inconsistency while the strategy is being implemented in the system.

Definition and installation of the strategy

Security policies must be captured in a format separate from the individual devices used to implement those policies. There are a few reasons to store this data outside of the implementing systems:
- Separate posting of the strategy allows the implementation to be audited by
  to the desired strategy.
- Policy definitions can be reused when switching the underlying application systems. For example, configuring a new vendor's system is made easier if the policy is captured in a non-vendor-specific format.

A separate database that captures planned policies can quickly become outdated unless mechanisms are put in place to ensure consistency with the implementation. The best way to do this is to generate an implementation configuration from this policy database using configuration management systems.

Some system administrators may choose to capture the policy directly in the configuration management code. In less mature networks, this approach is considered sufficient, as the configuration management system will consistently apply the defined policies on the target devices. As the network evolves, administrators may find that moving definitions to the data allows them to be used in more locations. For example, managed and host-based network firewalls can be configured from a shared policy database if that data is pulled from the configuration management code.

It is too difficult to define variable approval policies in less mature networks. Instead, system administrators should focus on defining and capturing known policies.

When developing policies, especially in an existing network, it is useful to have mechanisms to test proposed policies. "The gold standard" is a system that can take proposed policy changes and flag traffic that would be denied by implementing those policy changes. Building this policy preview system requires a number of components: a database of logged production flows, a policy simulator, and a system to identify differences in the current production policy and the proposed policy. For many organizations, this level of sophisticated policy simulation is simply out of reach.

A simpler approach to safely introducing policy changes can be achieved by using the following deployment procedure:

1. Take a subset of the desired policy, which we will call the proposed policy.
2. Deploy the proposed policy only in logging mode.
3. Collect production traffic over a sufficient period of time.
4. Investigate the traffic that would be rejected if the proposed policy were implemented.
5. Implement the proposed policy
6. Repeat this process until all desired rules have been deployed.
7. When all desired policies are in place, enable a policy that rejects traffic by default.

This "log then apply" procedure will provide sufficient time to detect unforeseen problems in the production environment. In addition to this approach, a phased deployment, where the policy is applied to a subset of the production footprint, can also help identify problems without affecting the entire production system.

Zero Trust Proxys

Zero Trust proxies are application proxy servers that can be used to secure a Zero Trust network. Proxies are deployed as infrastructure to manage authentication, authorization and encryption responsibilities. How these proxies are deployed is critical to ensuring the security of a Zero Trust network.

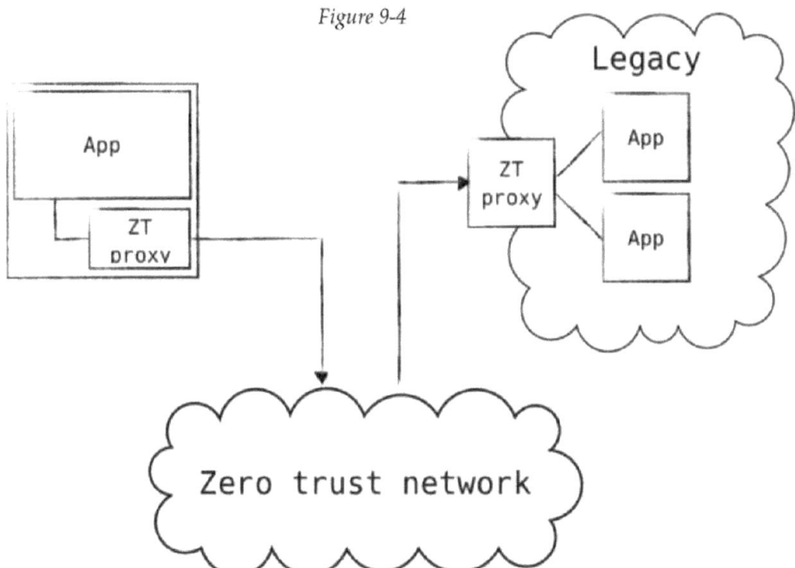

Zero Trust proxies can operate in two different modes: reverse proxy or direct proxy. Depending on the situation, one or both of these proxy modes can be used, as shown in Figure 9-4.

In reverse proxy mode, the proxy receives connection requests from zero-trust clients. The proxy receives the initial connection, validates that the connection should be allowed, and then forwards the request to the application for processing.

In direct proxy mode, a non-zero trust compliant component must make a network request to another Zero Trust system on the network. Since the non-zero trust compliant component is unable to work with the control plane to initiate the request properly, it communicates via the authentication proxy to handle this responsibility.

Proxies can be used to create a zero-trust network, but the proxies must be deployed on the same device that the workload is running on. When a zero-trust network is built in this manner, all workload communication is forcibly routed through the proxy before being sent out over the network. Isolating this responsibility in a proxy has advantages over embedding it in individual applications, which we discussed in Chapter 8.

It is not recommended to place proxies on dedicated devices to create a Zero Trust network. Trying to isolate zero trust responsibilities in an external proxy goes against the model that seeks to secure all traffic, including traffic between proxies/load balancers and backend services.

Creating a zero-trust network can be particularly difficult for system administrators who do not have full control over all devices or services on the network. For example, a network may have vendor-supplied components that need to be secured without changing the device itself.

Zero trust proxies can help fill the gap in this situation. Placing such a proxy between the unmodifiable component and the Zero Trust network can allow that component to participate in the network, but with less guarantee of its security.

It is essential that the non-zerotrust-aware component be completely isolated. This isolation must ensure that all network communications to and from this component can only occur via its authentication proxy. If possible, a direct mechanical connection should be preferred.

Client and server side migrations

When realizing a zero-trust network, deciding whether client-to-server or server-to-server interactions should be undertaken first ultimately depends on the needs of the organization and the level of effort required to achieve the goal.

Client-server interactions are usually the first to be targeted. Often, clients are physically mobile and access services from uncontrolled networks. Furthermore, with these devices being mobile, the physical security of the device is reasonably in question. So creating zero trust capabilities at this point of access brings a lot of value.

However, there are real barriers to building zero trust at the client/server layer. Organizations do not necessarily have automation systems installed on the client machines to enable the construction of the Zero Trust network. In addition, the types of devices used on clients can be much more diverse, which means that the required automation must be compatible with more systems.

Server-to-server interactions can be an easier initial target for zero-trust networks. These systems frequently have existing automation tools installed. They also tend to have a less diverse set of vendors. Finally, these are often the systems that host sensitive data and thus are an attractive target for potential attackers. Ultimately, the decision of where to start should focus on the target that is the weakest link in the system's network defenses. Building a threat model can help determine which systems are most at risk. With this knowledge, choosing where to invest time and resources is easier.

Chapter 10:
the view of the opponents

Most formal proposals in the technology industry include a section commonly referred to as "security considerations". In fact, the IETF requires a security considerations section for all submitted RFCs.

This section is crucial for several reasons. First, it clearly communicates potential pitfalls, hazards and warnings. This is extremely important during the implementation and deployment phases, as it ensures that the operator arrives at a design that retains the safety properties for which the system was originally designed.

Second, it shows that the author has thought through how the system can be attacked. It is far too easy to design a seemingly secure system that harbors a major vulnerability just below the surface. Finally, it sets the stage for a discussion on how best to address and manage the security risks presented. Therefore, including a section on security considerations is generally considered best practice. Some might even see the work as misleading without such a section, as it could indicate that the author is trying to push a known weak technology.

Even the strongest proposals will have security considerations. For example, the latest RFC for the TLS protocol is 12 pages long. It is important to understand that a system is not inherently insecure simply because there are security considerations associated with it; rather, it should indicate that the system as a whole is more secure.

In this chapter, we will discuss the potential pitfalls, dangers, and attack vectors associated with the zero trust model. If you were trying to penetrate a zero-trust network, how could you do it?

Identity theft

Virtually all decisions and transactions in a network of zero trust are made on the basis of authenticated identity. In Chapter 6, we discussed the difference between informal and authoritative identity, like the difference between your "human" identity and your government identity. Computer systems implement an authoritative identity similar to the way governments act - and in the same way that your government identity can be stolen, so can your identity in a computer system.

If your identity is stolen or compromised, an attacker could work his way through Zero Trust's authentication and authorization controls. This is, of course, extremely undesirable. Since identity in a computer system is typically tied to some sort of "secret" that is used to prove that identity, it is extraordinarily important to protect those secrets as well as possible.

These secrets can be protected in different ways, depending on the type of component to which the identity belongs. Special attention should be paid to choosing which methods to use for which components. We have discussed different ways to approach this problem in previous chapters.

Since a Zero-Trust network authenticates both the device and the user/application, it is necessary for an attacker to steal at least two identities to access resources, raising the bar over traditional approaches used today. These concerns can be mitigated by using behavioral analysis of the trust engine.

Although identity security is a widespread concern in the industry and is not specific to zero trust, its importance is significant enough to warrant its use, even though the zero trust model naturally mitigates this threat.

Distributed Denial Service

A zero-trust network is primarily concerned with authentication, authorization, and confidentiality, usually affected by strict access control to all network resources. While the architecture strives to authenticate and authorize just about everything on the network, it does not provide good mitigation against denial of service (DoS) attacks by itself. Distributed DoS attacks (DDoS) that are volumetric in nature can be particularly troublesome.

Just about any system that can receive packets is vulnerable to volumetric DDoS, even those using the zero-trust architecture. Some implementations "darken" Internet-connected endpoints through the use of pre-authentication protocols. We talked about this a bit in "Bootstrapping Trust: The First Packet", the basic principle being to hide these endpoints behind a deny-all rule, adding narrow exceptions based on signaling only. While this method helps keep endpoint addresses obscure, it does not fundamentally mitigate DDoS attacks.

Zero Trust networks, by nature, retain a great deal of information about what to expect on the network. This information can be used to calculate policy for more traditional traffic filtering defenses far upstream. For example, it may be that only a few systems on the network actually communicate with the Internet. In this case, we can use the policy to compute coarse-grained enforcement rules from the perspective of an upstream device, applying very broad enforcement with few exceptions. The advantages of this approach over the typical approach are twofold:
- The configuration is fully automated.
- Traffic filtering mechanisms can remain stateless.

The second advantage is quite important, as it avoids the need for expensive hardware and complicated state replication schemes. In this way, these filtering devices act more like scrubbers than firewalls. Of course, this only makes sense if you are running a large network. If you have some media in a colocation setup or have a native cloud, you may prefer to use an inline DDoS prevention service.

In short, DDoS is still a problem in the zero-trust world, and while we might have some smart new ways to address it, it will still require careful attention.

"Endpoint Enumeration

The zero-trust model naturally lends itself to perimeterless networks, as a perimeter makes much less sense when the internal network is untrusted. The peer-to-peer nature of perimeterless networks generally makes them easier to maintain than perimeter networks, which frequently include network gateways and tunnels such as VPNs that pose scalability, performance, and availability issues.

Because of this architecture, it is possible for an adversary to construct a system diagram by observing which systems communicate with which endpoints. This is in contrast to architectures that rely on network gateways such as VPNs, as an adversary observing VPN traffic cannot see conversations with endpoints beyond the VPN gateway. Note that this advantage is lost once traffic crosses the gateway - a classic property of the perimeter model.

This is where we make the distinction between privacy and confidentiality. The zero trust model guarantees network privacy, but not confidentiality. In other words, conversations in progress can be observed and claimed to exist; however, the content of the conversation is protected. Systems that provide network privacy attempt to hide the fact that the conversation took place. Tor is a popular example of a system that provides network privacy. This is a completely different problem space and is considered out of scope for the zero trust model.

If some limited form of privacy on public networks is desired, tunneling traffic via site-to-site tunnels remains an option in zero-trust networks. This deployment will make it more difficult to see which individual hosts are communicating on each side of the tunnel. We should be clear that this additional privacy protection should not be considered critical to network security. In fact, in some respects it undermines the zero-trust model itself, since hiding information in one part of the network and not another suggests that one is more trustworthy than the other.

Unreliable computer platform

We discussed this issue in Chapter 5, but it is important to reiterate that zero-trust networks require the underlying computing platform to be a trusted system.

There is a distinction to be made here between the computing platform itself (think cloud hardware, virtual machine hypervisor) is trusted and the "device" is trusted. Often these two systems are confused, but the attacks against each are subtly different because of their different levels of privilege.

Total defense against untrusted computing platforms is virtually impossible. Consider a system that uses hardware that deliberately generates weak random numbers (on which encryption systems depend). Defending against this type of attacker would involve first detecting the problem, although this may not be possible if the attacker is mostly hiding its capability.

Despite our inability to guard against a truly malicious computing platform, zero-trust systems can still guard against simpler attacks on the platform. Encrypting persistent data and exchanged memory pages will mitigate simpler attacks by malicious peers on the computing platform. It will also take away some trust from the platform operators and is therefore recommended.

Social engineering

Social engineering attacks, which trick trusted individuals into taking action on a trusted device, are always of great concern in zero-trust networks. Whether it's phishing attacks, non-malicious written communications, or face-to-face communications such as those faced by customer services, a zero-trust network can only defend attacks enabled by an unwitting participant.

For less sensitive resources, behavioral analysis of internal activity is the mechanism used to guard against this threat. This analysis is coupled with end-user training that teaches users to think like an adversary and to be wary of requests that are out of the ordinary.

For more sensitive assets, group authentication/authorization schemes like Shamir's secret sharing can help mitigate the effects of a single group member causing unexpected actions. This system can be very limiting on a day-to-day basis, so the best plan is to save it for truly critical assets.

Chapter 6 contains more details on these defense mechanisms against social engineering attacks.

Physical coercion

Zero Trust networks effectively mitigate many threats in the virtual world, but threats in the real world are another beast entirely. Valid users and devices can be effectively coerced to help an attacker gain access to a system they should not have access to. Border crossings can often be a place where government entities have significant power over someone who simply wants to get to their destination. And someone with a blunt instrument can force even the most honest individuals to help them.

The reality is that defending against these types of compromises is misguided. No security professional would tell someone in this situation to risk their physical well-being to protect the information they have access to. Therefore, the best we can do as an industry is to keep only the least sensitive data and systems vulnerable to compromise by a single individual. For higher value targets, group authorization is an effective mitigation measure against these threats.

Subtle physical attacks on individuals (say someone is able to insert a USB device into an unprotected laptop) are best mitigated by a consistent process of recycling devices and credentials. Scanning unconnected devices can also help mitigate these types of attacks.

If someone has physical access to your device, they can do a lot of damage. However, this statement should not be a license to throw up your hands and not at least try to mitigate these threats, especially when it comes to securing the data used for authentication/zero trust authorization. Clear steps can be taken to reduce the impact and duration of compromises, even if someone has physical access to a device, and zero-trust networks add these steps. You can read more about physical device security in Chapter 5.

Cancellation

Invalidation is a difficult problem in computer science. In the context of a zero-trust network, invalidation applies primarily to long-running actions that were previously authorized but are no longer so.

The definition of an action depends largely on the authorization processes you have chosen. For example, if you allow access on a request-by-request basis, an action will be considered a single application-level request/operation. If, on the other hand, you allow network flows (such as a TCP session) instead of application requests, an action will be considered a single network session.

The speed and efficiency with which ongoing actions can be invalidated profoundly affects the security response. It is important to assess the risk you are willing to tolerate in this area when designing your zero-trust network, as the response can have a significant impact on how you might approach certain problems. For example, if a new TCP session is the allowed action and some services maintain TCP sessions for several days, is it acceptable to say that an entity with revoked credentials can retain access for that period? Maybe not.

Fortunately, we have a few tools in our chest to solve this problem. First, and perhaps most obvious, is to perform more granular permissions on short-lived actions. Perhaps this means that the application component authorizes application-level requests instead of new network sessions. While it is still possible to have long-lived application requests, they are in practice less frequent than long-lived network sessions.

Another approach, although somewhat naive, is to periodically reset network sessions, imposing a maximum lifetime. When the application/client reconnects, it will be sent back through the authorization process.

However, the best approach is to teach the application component to track ongoing actions and, rather than resetting them after a period of time, send another authorization request to the rules engine. If the rules engine decides that the action is now unauthorized, the application component can forcibly reset it.

As you can see, these mechanisms are always based on a pull model, in which the application component is forced to periodically reauthorize. Therefore, sessions can only be invalidated as fast as the longest polling period configured in the application component. While invalidation is best done as a push or event-based model, these approaches have additional complexities and challenges that perhaps outweigh the benefits. Regardless, we can see that the problem is (at the very least) addressable.

Control plan security

We've discussed many control plane services throughout this book, responsible for things like policy authorization and inventory tracking. Depending on requirements, a zero-trust control plane can include a non-trivial number of services, all of which play a crucial role in ensuring authorization security across the network. A natural question follows: how can you protect your zero-trust control plane systems, and what happens if one is compromised?

Well, that's not good, that's for sure! It is possible to completely undermine the zero trust architecture if a control plane compromise is pervasive enough. As such, it is absolutely essential to ensure the security of these systems. This is not a weakness unique to the zero trust model - it still exists in perimeter networks today. If your perimeter firewall is compromised, what is the impact? Nevertheless, the concern is great enough to warrant discussion.

Control plane security can start with traditional means, providing very limited network connectivity and strict access control. Some control plane systems are more sensitive than others. For example, compromising a data store containing historical access data is strictly less useful to an attacker than compromising the policy engine. In the former case, an attacker may be able to artificially increase his trust level by falsifying access patterns, the latter resulting in a complete compromise of zero trust authorization, allowing the attacker to authorize anything he pleases.

For the most sensitive systems (i.e., the policy engine), strong controls must be applied from the beginning. Requiring group authentication and authorization to make changes to these systems is a real option and should be seriously considered. Changes should be infrequent and generate generalized messages or alerts. It should not be possible for a change in the control plan to go unnoticed.

Another good practice is to keep control plane systems isolated from an administrative standpoint. Perhaps this means they live in a dedicated cloud provider account or are kept in a part of the data center that has more stringent access control. This allows for a more thorough audit of access and minimizes the risk presented by administrative facilities to control plan systems. Isolating these systems administratively does not mean that they are logically isolated from the rest of the network. Despite administrative isolation, it is important that control plane systems participate in the network like any other service. Attempts to isolate them can quickly revert to a perimeter design, which can be considered the worst case scenario for zero-trust control plane security.

As the network matures, the application of zero trust can be slowly applied to the control plane systems themselves. Much like rewriting the C compiler in C, saving the application of zero-trust in the control plane ensures that security is applied consistently throughout the network and that there are no outliers. The propensity to introduce a chicken-and-egg problem should not deter you from this approach. Such problems are manageable and can usually be solved with enough thought. The alternative (putting control plane systems in a perimeter network) would leave those systems the least protected of all, and is generally unacceptable in the context of a zero-trust network.

Summary

This chapter attempts to approach the network of trust zero from the opposite perspective of the system administrators. By putting ourselves in the mindset of a potential attacker, we can evaluate the system as an adversary who has extensive knowledge of how it is set up.

Some of the attacks against zero-trust networks are well mitigated, while for others we can only detect the attack at best. Even a zero-trust network can be compromised by a determined adversary, because the disadvantage of defending against any theoretical attack is simply too high a price to pay in the day-to-day operation of such a network.

The reality is that every system is vulnerable to an attacker with sufficient resources. In the face of the most advanced attacks, the best we can hope for is effective and accurate detection. Starting from the premise that a system has been compromised and backing off to limit the damage is wise advice that could allow us to sleep soundly.

While the zero-trust model certainly introduces new considerations for networked system security, it also solves many more. By applying the power of automation to proven security protocols and primitives, the author is confident that the zero-trust model will grow to replace the perimeter model as a more efficient, scalable, and secure solution to the computer network security problem.

I want morebooks!

Buy your books fast and straightforward online - at one of world's fastest growing online book stores! Environmentally sound due to Print-on-Demand technologies.

Buy your books online at
www.morebooks.shop

Kaufen Sie Ihre Bücher schnell und unkompliziert online – auf einer der am schnellsten wachsenden Buchhandelsplattformen weltweit! Dank Print-On-Demand umwelt- und ressourcenschonend produzi ert.

Bücher schneller online kaufen
www.morebooks.shop

KS OmniScriptum Publishing
Brivibas gatve 197
LV-1039 Riga, Latvia
Telefax: +371 686 204 55

info@omniscriptum.com
www.omniscriptum.com

Printed by Books on Demand GmbH, Norderstedt / Germany